Carolyn
Stull

(510)
206-7802

Journeys
Through
ADDulthood

"{Sari Solden's} professional skill in helping others cope with ADD shines through in this well-organized, frankly stated work. . . . This important work stands out among the growing number of books on ADD . . ." —*Library Journal* (starred review)

"*Journeys Through ADDulthood* is, without question, one of the most important books on adult AD/HD since *Driven to Distraction*. Sari Solden has given us a blueprint to live our lives as adults with AD/HD, and has given therapists a book-length account of how to help their AD/HD adult clients. This is truly an awesome book!" —Arthur Robin, Ph.D., Professor of Psychiatry and Behavioral Neurosciences, Wayne State University

"Sari Solden has . . . expanded the sensitive, down-to-earth, practically oriented perspective she offered in *Women With Attention Deficit Disorder*. In this new volume, she offers women and men helpful understanding of the long, perplexing and often frustrating processes involved in coming to terms with AD/HD in oneself." —Thomas E. Brown, Ph.D., Associate Director, Yale Clinic for Attention & Related Disorders, Yale University School of Medicine.

"Solden's sense of humor and her anecdotes about her ongoing challenges with her own AD/HD flavor this book sweetly. She is one of the pioneers in the adult-AD/HD treatment community. . . . *Journeys Through ADDulthood* provides an important addition to the tool kits of clinicians working with AD/HD adults—regarding both understanding the disorder and treating it collaboratively with your clients. And your adult AD/HD clients will likely find great relief in Solden's mapping of the neurological, psychosocial, work and family issues and possible solutions connected with this terrain, terrain she continues to traverse herself." —reviewed in *The Therapist* by Ellen Patterson

"Solden emphasizes reconnecting with the dreams that unexplained AD/HD symptoms may have prematurely cut off. With the spark of discovering who one really is, and recognizing one's strengths again, in the context of these challenges, Solden envisages a new life for AD/HD adults which goes way beyond discovering how many milligrams of this or that one must take." —reviewed in the CHADD of Northern California newsletter by Lew Mills, MFT, Ph.D.

Sari Solden

Journeys
Through
ADDulthood

Discover a New Sense of
Identity and Meaning
While Living with
Attention Deficit Disorder

WALKER & COMPANY
NEW YORK

I dedicate this book to all the brave women and men with whom I have worked over the years and from whom I have learned to honor and respect the struggle as well as appreciate the gifts that differences can bring.

First published in the United States of America in 2002 by Walker Publishing Company, Inc.

Published simultaneously in Canada by Fitzhenry and Whiteside, Markham, Ontario L3R 4T8

For information about permission to reproduce selections from this book, write to Permissions, Walker & Company, 435 Hudson Street, New York, New York 10014

Library of Congress Cataloging-in-Publication Data available upon request
ISBN 0-8027-1376-9
ISBN 0-8027-7679-5 (paperback)

Visit Walker & Company's Web site at www.walkerbooks.com

Illustrations on pages xviii, 11, 12, 14, 28, 39, 54, 57, 59, 73, 89, 124, and 183 are by David Zinn.

Book design by Dede Cummings Designs

Printed in the United States of America

10 9 8 7 6 5 4 3 2

Contents

Journey Three:
Crisis of Success—
Focus: Your "Self" in the World

Foreword

WHEN SARI SOLDEN asked me to write a foreword to this book, I gladly accepted. She's one of the wisest, warmest people I know, so it is my privilege to add a few words to her wonderful new book.

· If you are just picking this book up, you are probably doing so for one of two reasons: Either you know Sari's previous work and want to read more by her, or you do not know of Sari but you want to learn more about Attention Deficit Disorder in adults. Either way, you have made a good choice. I recommend the book most highly.

Before you begin, allow me to offer a few observations about ADD, or AD/HD—what diagnosis and treatment can do for adults.

You may be wondering, Is it ADD or AD/HD? As of now, the diagnostic term is *AD/HD*, Attention Deficit Hyperactivity Disorder. However, you can have AD/HD without having the symptom of hyperactivity. Indeed, you could be a serene daydreamer, just the opposite of hyperactive. So you can have AD/HD without the *H*. We see this commonly in girls and women, but it also can occur in boys and men.

It wasn't too long ago that no one had heard of AD/HD. I myself had not heard of it until 1981, when I was starting my fellowship in child psychiatry. Before then, if you had told me there was a disorder characterized by a deficit of attention, I would have thought this was some psychoanalytic term related to people who did not receive enough nurturing or attention when they were young.

But in 1981 I learned better. Not only did I learn what AD/HD is, I learned that I have it myself. Naturally, I became very interested in it and went on to write a couple of books about it along with my friend, John Ratey.

Now, some twenty years later, most people have heard of AD/HD. But most people still do not know exactly what it is. This book will help clarify the issue.

The reason that it is important to know about AD/HD is that proper diagnosis and treatment can change your life dramatically for the better, no matter what your age. The oldest person I treated was eighty-six, and she said the treatment improved her life, among other ways, by allowing her to play with her great-grandchildren without getting distracted and to read aloud to them. She felt a tremendous gratitude to me for giving her back her great-grandchildren, not to mention her many friends and other relatives.

We do not know exactly what AD/HD is, but we are learning more and more all the time. Brain research is advancing rapidly, and new methods of more accurately diagnosing AD/HD are close at hand. In addition, new forms of treatment are being developed as the research continues to grow.

It is important to think of AD/HD as a kind of mind, one that you were born with and will continue to live with forever. You should look not for a cure but for a method of managing your mind most effectively. The goal of treatment should not only be to minimize the negative symptoms of AD/HD but, even more important, to identify and develop the talents you have. Too often the life story of an adult with AD/HD is a long story of struggle, with few victories and many defeats. Treatment should not merely aim to stave off more defeats but also aim to promote many victories.

The kinds of victories adults with AD/HD can reasonably expect depend upon what kind of mind a given adult has. AD/HD is only a descriptor; it does not define a person. So treatment should begin by taking a look at the entire human being—you—and finding out what talents might lead to which victories.

People with AD/HD are often just one or two changes away from a much happier life. The change might be a new job, or a new exercise regimen, or a new understanding of who you are and how you got this way. One of the most important changes is to understand yourself in medical as opposed to moral terms. Most adults with AD/HD carried in their hearts before they got diagnosed what amounted to a "moral diagnosis," such as being "bad" or "irresponsible." When you replace that moral diagnosis with the correct medical diagnosis, AD/HD, you can start to lift the burden of self-condemnation off yourself. You can stand up tall, at last, and you can live up to what all along you had dimly perceived you were capable of.

The victories that can ensue are not only related to work and professional success. They are also victories in your personal life. You can learn how to sustain a close relationship. You can learn that your problem all along has not been a problem with intimacy but difficulty lingering over any moment. If you can never linger—over coffee, over a sunset, over a remark, over a kiss—then it is hard to get close to anyone.

You may also find that you can play with your children in a more focused way, or with your great-grandchildren! You may find the company of your friends more fulfilling, less tedious. You may find reading a book less of a chore; you might even look forward to reading! You might find that you can clean up your desk and finally set up a filing system that works. You might excavate all your piles. You might wear socks that match every day, and even learn how to be on time.

Your victories might come over internal, emotional states. You might begin to control your anger more effectively, or give in to impatience less vociferously. You might find that boredom no longer makes you want to SCREAM, and that waiting in line is not tantamount to having bamboo shoots shoved under your fingernails.

You might begin to score the victory of finding meaning in your life, of finding continuity from one day to the next, one week to the next, one month to the next, and one year to the next. You might develop an internal definition of who you are, and might actually feel comfortable with it. You might start to like yourself. And you might find that others start to like you better as well.

You might begin to quiet that incessant critic inside who has been eating away at your soul for as long as you can remember. You might find yourself laughing more and learning a new skill called "relaxing."

Your sex life might improve. How? Did you ever consider how paying truly close attention is related to making love well?

Your physical health might improve. Treatment of AD/HD often reduces all kinds of somatic complaints, from low-back pain to nonspecific headache syndromes to digestive troubles, to skin rashes, and on and on.

I have seen people achieve all of these victories and many others. That is why I love to treat adults who have AD/HD. They change for the better, and they change quickly.

Sari Solden will guide you through the journey of change. She is a learned, insightful, and compassionate guide. If you stay with her and read this book, you might just find the life you have been seeking for a very long while. You won't find a perfect life; no one finds that. But you might find the better life you have always known could be yours, if only you could find the key. This book might be that key.

> Edward Hallowell, M.D., director of the Hallowell Center
> in Sudbury, Massachusetts; instructor in psychiatry at
> Harvard Medical School; and author of eight books,
> including *Driven to Distraction, Worry, Connect,*
> and *Human Moments*

Preface

I HAVE WRITTEN THIS BOOK for adults coping with Attention Deficit Hyperactivity Disorder, whether in therapy or out, with or without medication. For more than twelve years I've worked as a therapist with adults living with the differences and difficulties of AD/HD. During this time I have witnessed the struggle that goes far beyond the management of primary symptoms. I have come to understand that once a diagnosis is made and the symptoms are stabilized, a new challenge emerges: to reclaim your life, find a new purpose, and reshape the dreams that you may have buried. I've had the opportunity to see the exciting period of relief and hope that follows diagnosis. I also have been struck by the complexity of both the feelings and the challenges that continue to present themselves to people with AD/HD far beyond diagnosis and medication, even with good early treatment.

This book is for both men and women. Ever since my first book, *Women with Attention Deficit Disorder,* was published in 1995, a great number of men have confided to me that many of the feelings I expressed in that book were their feelings, too, and needed to be given expression as well.

There is a thread that unites most adults with AD/HD, especially those who were undiagnosed until adulthood.

Many of the effects described in this book come as a result of not understanding the challenges of AD/HD during one's formative years.

In addition, I have written this book to address what seems to me the growing polarization in the field of adult AD/HD. The following questions speak to that divide. Is AD/HD a curse or a blessing? Is AD/HD to be judged only by external, measurable symptoms or by inner experiences as well? When people who have AD/HD are successful, is it because or in spite of their difficulties? Is a person still disabled if she or he is above average? Is AD/HD the province of research scientists or clinicians? Who is authorized to say who has it and who doesn't?

In my opinion, the adults with AD/HD, the researchers, and the clinicians each have a piece of the truth from their different viewpoints. Clinicians, like myself, who see adults in private practice often tend to see gifted or creative adults with AD/HD, whereas some of the professionals working in different settings may see a different population.

We must not dismiss the difficulties and the sometimes disabling effects of AD/HD. We also must not lose sight of the entire person. Peter Jaksa, former president of the National Attention Deficit Disorder Association (ADDA), expressed this idea eloquently in his article "Flowers and Thorns and Roses" in the Fall 1999 issue of *Focus* magazine. He wrote: "The researchers might look at the symptoms of ADD and see primarily thorns while others with a more humanistic view might say that thorns are simply part of the larger whole and need to be regarded seriously and dealt with realistically, but without being mistaken as the primary feature of the rose bush or the feature that gives the rose bush its purpose and defines its identity."

I believe we must bring humanism and science together. The challenge at this point in the field of adult AD/HD, when so many have now been diagnosed for several years, is to expand the focus on biochemistry to include an examination of how living with a particular brain function affects the development of one's view of self. Working on the self is not just a "feel-good" piece of the AD/HD puzzle. On the contrary, it is very often the critical link, which in the long run makes the difference between those adults who are able to utilize all the medical and scientific advances and those who are not.

This book takes the reader on three journeys through "ADDulthood." Before providing a preview of these journeys in the next section, I want to say a few words of explanation about the terms and devices used in the volume.

Attention Deficit/Hyperactivity Disorder (AD/HD) is the term currently accepted by the professional community, regardless of whether one's struggles include hyperactivity, so I have used it throughout the book, except in the title and subtitle. Quotes using Attention Deficit Disorder (ADD) have been left in their original form. I use the term *treatment* in the broadest sense. It does not signify medical treatment, or even counseling on a regular long-term basis, although both might be necessary supports at times. Treatment refers to how an adult "treats" him- or herself, in or out of these more standard therapies.

Throughout this book, there are self-help exercises, or "explorations," at the end of each chapter. They are designed to help you decide where you are in your travels and what roadblocks you still need to get around in order to progress. At the end of the book there are recommended resources for further exploration. A special section (appendix B) is provided for mental health professionals and others who want more information on counseling adults with AD/HD.

I tell the story of two men and two women in great detail. They are composites of numerous people I have known and worked with, and represent a synthesis of many of the major struggles and styles of adults with AD/HD. Any resemblance to a particular person is purely coincidental. The descriptions of each character's challenges can apply equally to a man or a woman. (Note: This book doesn't attempt to describe all adults with AD/HD, especially those who struggle with other disorders in addition to their attention difficulties.)

Journeys Through ADDulthood

Before starting on any voyage, you must have some fundamental knowledge. You need to know where you're going, what to look for, which choices to make, and what signs to recognize that will point you in right direction. This book will be your travel guide, sharing with you what I've learned about AD/HD and what I've discovered from other travelers. It is my hope that this book will make the road a little easier for you and help you identify and circumvent any roadblocks.

If after diagnosis and treatment you are feeling lost or stuck, I will show you the detours and exciting side trips, and recommend good company. If you are headed for trouble, I'll point this out to you. Bear in mind that if you have gone off track for a long time, it will take a while to find your way back to the road; don't try to make up for lost time by going too fast or taking shortcuts, because that may be counterproductive. Although you can't go back and start over, you can reassess your goals and find a new route that is not a dead end or filled with obstacles.

This book describes three journeys, or stages of development, that will lead you to a more satisfying life—even with AD/HD. They are not quick fixes or "easy lessons" to be memorized and applied all at once. Instead, they are elements of an ongoing process, which takes a longer view of the challenges that will present themselves and the experiences you will need in order to successfully navigate through the uncharted waters of your life.

In each stage there is a crisis point, defined as a critical turning point, a change toward either improvement or deterioration. At every crisis point there are key issues that should be resolved in order to move forward. When they are left unresolved, you remain stuck. There also are essential tasks that must be integrated as the building blocks of "ADDult" development.

Prediagnosis is labeled here as a "Crisis of Confusion" where the focus of your life is on your deficits. Journey One begins at diagnosis and becomes a "Crisis of Understanding," because knowing that you have AD/HD shakes up your entire worldview and brings into question, as well as into bold relief, your lifelong experiences. It may fill you with grief and loss, as well as hope and relief. The focus of treatment in Journey One is on the primary symptoms of AD/HD, with the goal of maximizing your brain's effectiveness and reducing your most troublesome symptoms.

In Journey Two the emphasis of treatment moves necessarily from your brain to your view of your self and your differences from other people. The goal is to correct your

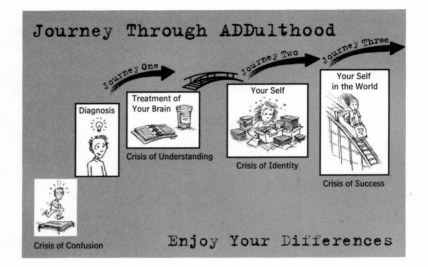

Journey Through ADDulthood

Journey One → Journey Two → Journey Three

Diagnosis

Treatment of Your Brain
Crisis of Understanding

Your Self
Crisis of Identity

Your Self in the World
Crisis of Success

Crisis of Confusion

Enjoy Your Differences

distorted self-view and resolve the ensuing Crisis of Identity in order to arrive at a new vision of yourself and your future. When you have done this you will start to experience a sense of purpose, and excitement, *even though you continue to struggle with many of the primary symptoms of AD/HD.*

Journey Three is about learning to take care of and protect yourself so you can share who you are with others—without sacrificing your vitality, newly awakened dreams, or positive feelings you have worked so hard to achieve. The focus at this point is on maintaining your sense of self while in relationships and while enjoying your place in the world.

Eventually, you measure success not just by external, observable progress but by internal rewards: feelings of satisfaction and freedom, including the freedom to make your own choices. That is the ultimate goal of this truly wonderful journey.

Journeys
Through
ADDulthood

Introduction:
"Meanwhile, I Keep Dancing"

I get up.

I walk.

I fall down.

Meanwhile, I keep dancing.

—RABBI HILLEL

WHEN I READ THIS SIMPLE QUOTE by Rabbi Hillel, I was struck in the deepest way by how it summed up what I had been searching for a way to express for some time. It put words to the voyage I had witnessed hundreds of adults with AD/HD—including myself—take over the last twelve years. People who, after a diagnosis of and initial treatment for AD/HD, have gone on to live satisfying lives tend to be able to separate who they are from their AD/HD difficulties and differences, to distinguish between their worth as people and the problems that threaten to engulf them on a daily basis.

This struggle, captured so poignantly in Hillel's few lines, is not about minimizing the difficulties or idealizing the differences. It is about continuing to struggle while being of two minds, and on two simultaneous paths. It is about continuing the lifelong challenge of keeping your hopes, dreams, spirit, and real self alive and well while struggling with adult AD/HD.

Over the years, I've given many speeches on the topic of AD/HD. I often begin a talk by sharing one of several stories about my own struggle with AD/HD—to disabuse people of the notion that there is one kind of end point; to remind them that there isn't a linear progression from AD/HD to non-AD/HD. I want to share the following story with you for the same reasons. Even though for a long time I had thought that I accepted my AD/HD, a recent experience brought very deep feelings to the surface and forced me to reevaluate basic questions about my differences from others and my own self-worth.

My husband and I adopted a ten-year-old girl from Russia after meeting and falling in love with her one summer a few years ago. After this initial meeting we had to go through a serious decision-making process that had a great deal to do with my AD/HD. Even though I have a biological son who is now grown, I did not know I had AD/HD before he was born, so it was not a consideration. Now I was faced with knowing extremely well the challenges of my AD/HD. I asked myself how my AD/HD would be affected by adopting this girl and, more important, what impact my AD/HD would have on her. I struggled with the question of what the essential qualities of being a good parent are, as do many parents with AD/HD. For me, I worried about baking, cooking, and disorganization, whereas others might struggle with such activities as getting a child to school on time. Would it be fair to her if I became her mother? What did I have to offer?

Friends and family assured me I had many wonderful inner qualities to offer, but I was so focused on my more visible liabilities that I wasn't able at the time to see my true value as a parent. While my concerns were understandable, they certainly wouldn't disqualify a person from being a good and loving parent. Although I've been able to advise others to value their strengths just as much as their deficits, I couldn't seem to apply this advice to my own circumstances. When it came to the stark reality of such a life-altering decision, all I could do was shift back and forth between two images: this child in Russia in an orphanage versus my omnipresent piles of papers (a common AD/HD hallmark). I was having a very hard time figuring out how much weight to give these different realities.

Then at one point someone I know, who wasn't trying to be mean but was just wondering, asked me bluntly: "Do you think she will be able to tolerate you?" I pictured my future daughter far away in her orphanage and then me and my piles, and immediately I recognized how absurd the question was. At that moment I could see clearly all that I had to offer this child.

Whereas a question like that might have made me upset or defensive or depressed at an earlier point in my AD/HD travels, this time I was able to laugh. Even a few years before, even after diagnosis, I would have felt too inadequate to take on this huge endeavor. I wouldn't have seen or appreciated that my strengths at least equaled my difficulties. This, of course, doesn't mean they cancel them out. I wasn't soft-pedaling my difficulties or pretending they would not have an impact. I just tried to use all the information about who I am as a whole person. I tried to be realistic about the impact the adoption would have; I prepared myself emotionally and got enough physical support for this difficult but exhilarating challenge.

And so my husband and I went halfway around the world to bring back our new daughter.

Now at night when I hold my daughter, I look around at the disarray that at times surrounds us, and I add a little something to a favorite line of mine by Ralph Waldo Emerson (my addition is in italics): "What lies behind us and what lies before us (*and what lies around us*) are tiny matters compared to what lies within us."

There is a postscript to this story. My daughter had been with us a year when she turned to me at the airport as I was leaving to go to speak at a national AD/HD conference. She was frustrated at my not being able to find my ID for the fourth time that day. She looked me straight in the eye and said, "Mom, you're a messy person!" I braced myself and thought, "OK, here it comes. This is what I knew would happen someday. Now is the test of my theory about what is truly important against reality." I asked her as calmly as possible to tell me how big a problem this is to her. I also told her I was soon going to be talking to a big group of messy people. "What would you have me tell them about this?" I asked her. Again she looked me straight in the eye and said, "Tell them it's not important. What's important is how you feel about me and who you are inside."

Critical Turning Points

In every individual I have seen who goes on to live a satisfying life with AD/HD, there is a critical shift at some point after initial treatment.

As a therapist, I began to watch for these shifts, or internal markers, and started to realize they were points where people crossed a threshold, pushing through their internal barriers to continue to meet their shifting challenges. I became aware that some people were able to keep moving along in their inner voyage while others were becoming stuck. I listened as people shared descriptions of themselves, their relationships, and of their own differences. The details of individual stories were different, but the themes and markers represented in their continued growth and development after diagnosis were the same in significant ways.

I continued to use this model and realized there was a continuum of progress. When a new client told me her story, I could quickly recognize where she was on this continuum. And when I had been working with someone for an extended period, at some point I could perceive the shift in her development. This progress wasn't measured by how organized her life was. Instead it was a measure of her

You don't get over the struggle with AD/HD, but you can separate yourself and your self-view from your primary symptoms. At this point you move on with your life, even though the symptoms continue to give you difficulty. Your yardstick of success must include inner experiences as well as more conventional markers. Your goal is not "normalcy," but rather to become comfortable with yourself.

self-image and her ability to "get on with life anyway," to form a postdiagnosis identity, and to sustain close relationships despite her continuing AD/HD symptoms.

The AD/HD component of your life has to be continually dealt with, but it's not your whole self; nor should overcoming AD/HD be your overall goal or destination. AD/HD contributes a greater deal to your voyage—its struggles, storms, beauty. The goal is to embrace your true identity, to enjoy and derive satisfaction from your life despite the difficulties of AD/HD. The great challenge is to "keep dancing," even while continuing to struggle.

Crisis of Understanding—
Focus: Your Brain

1

Living in Two Different Worlds

Understanding Your Differences

ATTENTION DEFICIT HYPERACTIVITY DISORDER is a biochemical brain disorder resulting in a range of severe and chronic symptoms. In general, people who have this syndrome may have difficulty directing and maintaining their attention, may be impulsive and easily distracted by both external and internal stimuli.

In real life, the disorder is far more complicated than that. Adults with Attention Deficit Hyperactivity Disorder (AD/HD) may talk fast, interrupt others in conversation, do too many things at once, rush through activities, and act on impulses without adequate assessment of consequences. Those who have what is presumably called Attention Deficit Hyperactivity Disorder, Inattentive Type, are not hyperactive and may actually be shy and withdrawn during childhood, more likely to daydream, and be lost in an inner world. As adults, they may have trouble rallying themselves to get started or take action. They may work and process information more slowly than do others of equal education,

EXECUTIVE FUNCTIONING

"Executive functions are management functions of the mind," explains Thomas Brown, noted psychologist and AD/HD expert from Yale University. "They activate, regulate, and integrate a wide variety of other mental functioning. An individual's ability to perform many important daily tasks of school, work, family, and social interaction may be markedly impaired relative to others of the same age and mental development. While everyone has problems sometimes, ADD adults have significant chronic impairments that are persistent and more pervasive than their peers." These impairments include "severe difficulty in mobilizing and sustaining . . . attention, alertness, effort, and working memory functions for less interesting, though important tasks."* Brown goes on to say that what confuses observers is that ADD impairments are chronic but not constant. In many cases, other family members will mistakenly attribute these physical symptoms of the ADD adult to a moral or character flaw, such as irresponsibility, immaturity, selfishness, or a problem with motivation.

ability, or intelligence. (It is now recognized that impairments of executive functions of the brain are a core problem of AD/HD; see boxed text above.)

Many adults have a mixture of these symptoms, which often results in disorganization in their lives. The external manifestations may be forgotten appointments, missed deadlines, a disheveled desk, or a messy home. Some people also feel disorganized on the inside. Whichever type of AD/HD you have as an adult, you may feel socially isolated,

---

* Thomas Brown, "New Understandings of Attention Deficit Disorder in Children, Adolescents, and Adults: Assessment and Treatment," *Focus: The Official Newsletter of the National Attention Deficit Disorder Association*, Fall 1999, 3, 12.

discouraged, and frustrated by underachievement and over-whelmed by the difficulties of everyday life.

The Basics of AD/HD Treatment

Throughout your life you will always need to review the treatment for your primary AD/HD symptoms and the care of your brain. No matter what else you are working through at any point in your life after diagnosis, always start with a check of your current "state of mind." Whenever symptoms appear to be causing new or more severe problems, you need to go through an internal checkup, asking yourself such questions as: Is my medication still working, or do I need a new consultation? Do I have enough support in place? What in my life has gotten out of hand? What needs adjusting?

Understanding how your AD/HD brain works marks the beginning of Journey One, the "Crisis of Understanding." It is a crucial part of the internal stage of treatment. There are many excellent sources that describe, in depth, the treatment for primary symptoms of AD/HD. (Some suggestions are provided in the "Recommended Resources" section of this book.) For the person getting acquainted with AD/HD for the first time, here is is a brief guide to primary treatment

from my perspective. The following MESST model for the treatment of AD/HD stands for Medication, Education, Support, Strategies, and Therapy. Much of this section, especially "The Grief Cycle," is taken from my previous book, Women with Attention Deficit Disorder.

When I say treatment, I mean basically whatever helps you. It might include (although it doesn't have to) individual psychotherapy, medication, coaching, group support, or couples counseling. The following combinations of tools are effective ways to help you manage your primary AD/HD symptoms.

MEDICATION

AD/HD symptoms are most commonly linked to the inefficient transmission of information in the brain, through chemical brain messengers called neurotransmitters. Neurotransmitters send information between the millions of nerve cells in the brain. Medication works on these neurotransmitters by making them more available where they are needed, thus "smoothing out" the transmission of information in the brain, and consequently leveling off AD/HD symptoms. For many adults with AD/HD, medication is the fuel that allows the brain to function more smoothly and efficiently. Medication doesn't cure everything, but it often gives you the focus to be able to strategize effectively and engage support, and to stay on track in order to make your life work again.

Stimulants, such as Ritalin, Dexadrine, Adderall, and Concerta, are commonly prescribed medications for adults with AD/HD. In addition, many individuals have been treated effectively with a combination of stimulants and antidepressants. The correct medication can increase alertness and focus, and regulate activity levels. It also can give you sustained energy and reduce your emotional reactivity and distractibility. It can help to reduce your anxiety and lessen your response to each new distracting or interesting idea that appears to you, making it easier for you to filter out the internal and external information that may be bombarding you. It can provide a cushion so you don't feel as sensitive, open, or raw. Not only can medication help with school or work or organizing, but it may also allow you to be able to stay with a conversation and to interact and connect with people in a new way.

For some people, the effect of prescribed medication is dramatic to them and others. Sometimes people know within a few hours that the medication is making a tremendous difference. They feel awake and alert for the first time in their lives—as if they're coming out of a fog.

On the other hand, you may not feel dramatically different. It could take months before you can look back and see that your life has improved in significant ways. For instance, you may have accomplished more, you may have stayed on track, or your relationships may have improved.

AD/HD medication has been proven to be very safe and effective when monitored and prescribed by an experienced doctor. Before you start using a particular medication, it's a good idea to take the time to read enough about it to ask informed questions during your "meds" consultation. The more you know before you talk to the doctor, the more assertive you can be if you feel your concerns aren't being adequately addressed. It is valuable to talk to a mental health professional who has experience with adults with AD/HD, who can track the effects of the medication, and who will be accessible and responsive to your questions about what is happening and what can be expected. You may experience a wide range of feelings associated with your medication. You may have to work out feelings of being disappointed, wondering, "Is this all I can expect?" or "What do I need to do now in addition to taking the medication?"

EDUCATION

Information about subjects such as organizational strategies, medication, and the brain is essential in order to give you a thorough explanation for what you experience with AD/HD. It can also provide a solid foundation in how to manage your life. I recommend you take advantage of

 whatever is available in your area, as well as the recommended resources at the end of this book. Attend lectures and conferences, which provide information on such topics as medication, neuropsychology, the grief cycle, emotions, relationship issues, strategies, and coping techniques.

Education can provide great emotional healing as well as information. By providing a link to the experiences of others similar to yours, either in person or through reading, it helps

you overcome your isolation. Knowing that others have gone through similar experiences can have a soothing effect. Education helps relieve anxiety and self-doubt, because it takes a long time for people to consistently and deeply believe they have AD/HD. It is good to get this idea reinforced from those who are positive about it—coping and living well with AD/HD. Education will give you the advantage of hearing these subjects talked about for the first time.

Join organizations such as ADDA (the national Attention Deficit Disorder Association), CHADD (Children and Adults with ADD), and support groups that deal with adults, and subscribe to pertinent newsletters or magazines (especially if you don't attend a group). It is very important to associate with other adults with AD/HD, either in person or through reading their stories. A number of newsletters and magazines are listed in the "Recommended Resources" section, ranging from those that are research-oriented to those that are more chatty. Here you will read about other people's experiences and all the latest news about AD/HD workshops and conferences. The Internet also can provide wonderful connections with other adults.

There are some very good conferences for adults with AD/HD, sponsored by ADDA, CHADD, and ADDIEN (ADD Information Exchange Network). A conference is a great way for those with AD/HD to spend time with hundreds of other people who are not hiding anymore, who are talking about all the things they have experienced. You will see people from all walks of life, some of whom have been dealing with AD/HD for a long time, and some who are just starting out. Attending a conference can be an important first step in alleviating some of the old feelings of shame and guilt and isolation.

THE AD/HD COACH

"Individuals with AD/HD are often aware that they must design their environment so they will be productive and have the proper reminders built in," say Susan Sussman and Nancy Ratey, two founders of the AD/HD coaching movement. "Using people like supervisors and spouses as coaches often generates feelings of inadequacy and frustration due to the nature of these relationships. The coach is an emotionally neutral person in the life of an individual with AD/HD. The strong feelings that may be attached to a spouse or supervisor are absent in the coaching relationship. Thus the coach can offer suggestions and reminders, provide structure and boundaries and be perceived by the client as helpful and supportive. Coaching can be the client's way of designing an environment that meets his own unique needs."

SUPPORT

During the early stages of your AD/HD travels, it's often difficult for your family to accept and understand your AD/HD. They have their own emotional issues to work through, so they may not be able to provide the support you need. This increases your sense of isolation and frustration.

It's essential that you start to receive emotional support from other people who can provide a positive environment, such as counselors, coaches, and support groups. When you join a support group, you will no longer feel so isolated, and input from the group can help you gain strengths, develop strategies, and take the risks that will ultimately improve your life.

You also need physical support, which means arranging to have people around you to help with the physical details of life that are hard for you. I don't recommend that you cope with these details alone. People newly diagnosed with AD/HD often say, "Now that I know about this, I'm going to go home and I'm going to try harder." Doing the same thing you've always done, but "trying harder," just sets you up for frustration. Such determination is admirable, but it does not take into consideration the whole picture. AD/HD requires that you make accommodations in order to make progress. That includes getting the necessary level of support from other people. With each new success, you might need to go to a new level of physical support. You will, in time, need to rethink how you're going to set up your life. You will actually negotiate with partners, you will trade tasks with friends, or you will consider hiring help in the specific areas where you need it.

STRATEGIES

Although closely related to physical support, strategies are more about thinking through how to set up your environment in a way that works for you. You may use a variety of technological and other devices. Strategizing effectively means taking into account your real-life difficulties and setting things up so that you have a better chance to succeed.

Here are examples of strategies that could help you manage your life more efficiently.

- **Plan enough time between activities to give yourself downtime.**

- **Try the night before to prepare or gather what you will need the next morning, when it will be harder for you to think.**

- **Allow much more time to process information in between activities.**

- **If you are in college, try to arrange a balanced courseload in terms of hours and work required in various classes.**

- **At work, consider the use of sound blocks to create a nondistracting environment for yourself.**

- **When you're busy and don't want to be interrupted, let voice mail or an answering machine record your phone calls, which you can listen to at your convenience.**

THERAPY

Therapy or counseling can play an important role in the overall treatment for AD/HD. As with depression or anxiety, medication and therapy together are generally more effective than either is alone. Some of the issues that arise for adults with AD/HD in counseling include shame, depression, self-image, and relationship issues. Counseling can take place with individuals, couples, or groups.

In therapy, you may be helped to understand that after diagnosis it is normal to grieve and begin working through a grief cycle. While this term is usually applied to life-threatening events, it is now recognized that having AD/HD is a life-altering, identity-changing experience.

I often think of AD/HD as a subculture of its own, one that operates according to its own rules and modes of communication. Anyone who has been at an AD/HD adult conference knows there is a big cultural divide between the AD/HD and non-AD/HD worlds. Those with AD/HD

THE GRIEF CYCLE

Denial

Denial may follow the period of relief that can accompany diagnosis. At first you might either deny the reality of AD/HD or accept it superficially but continue to question if it really applies to you. Even if you say you have AD/HD, you may have not yet integrated it in any kind of deep or meaningful way that will help you adjust. Even after diagnosis, when your AD/HD symptoms emerge, you may attribute them to personal failings: "I'm stupid and irresponsible." As with any new life-altering event or change of self-view, the person diagnosed with AD/HD often goes through an initial period of shock.

Anger

After you understand that you do have something called AD/HD, you begin to look back and see how deeply it has affected every area of your life. At this point, you may become angry over lost opportunities. You may focus on the point at which things started to go off course and begin to feel anger toward those who let you down as a child: family members who didn't help, teachers who misunderstood, or people who blamed you. Or you may just feel angry in general that this is happening, that life has been so hard. It is helpful for you to see that anger is a natural part of the grief cycle and that it is important and necessary to experience it in order to move beyond it and continue in a positive direction.

Bargaining

When people understand that they have AD/HD, they are naturally encouraged and excited to learn that medication can help. They say, "OK, I have AD/HD, but I'll just take my medication and I'll be all right." They figure that taking medication will take care of the AD/HD. Unfortunately, medication for AD/HD is not a magic pill and usually is not sufficient alone as treatment. Because the benefits of medication don't always match a person's expectations, disappointment and discouragement often set in.

Depression

When the medication doesn't cure everything, when even though you feel better and many areas of your life are greatly improved, you still have many of the same difficulties, you may begin to feel depressed. Your difficulties can be seen as even harder at this point because the whole experience can be so disorganizing in and of itself. You're caught between two worlds for a while. You want to forget about AD/HD and go back to the way things were. Even if your old system didn't work very well, at least it was familiar. You've seen other people with AD/HD and by now you know that there's a long road ahead, but the process seems like too much to deal with. Maybe you are not yet getting enough of the support that would make it easier to make necessary changes; therefore, you feel isolated and lonely, which also contributes to feelings of depression.

Acceptance

With the right kind of support, counseling, and education, or merely with the passage of time, most people eventually move to acceptance. However, some people keep going through the other phases of the grief cycle without reaching acceptance; others may move to acceptance and then go through the entire cycle again. At the end of Journey One, it is common to achieve what I call a false acceptance, or pseudo-acceptance. The point of true acceptance comes later, when you will have integrated in a deep way the idea of yourself as a person with AD/HD. You stop thinking of AD/HD as a weakness of willpower or a moral failure. Instead, you accept that although you can manage your AD/HD symptoms, they will still exist. And you recognize your responses to the AD/HD and modify them so your internal and external reactions don't make things worse. Acceptance is much more difficult to achieve than is commonly thought. While you may have accepted the reality, it takes a much longer time to achieve true self-acceptance, to be able to live fully and richly—AD/HD and all.

come together and share their stories, their experiences, and create a comfortable and safe environment where they can easily understand one another in a way that is not possible in the larger, non-AD/HD world. For example, at an AD/HD conference, no one would make a fuss over spilling a drink, whereas in the non-AD/HD world the person who spilled would apologize and feel embarrassed. In the non-AD/HD world, interrupting and completing the sentences of others is often seen as rude and inconsiderate. At an AD/HD conference, however, this sort of interaction is the norm and part of the fun. Likewise, suddenly changing the subject of conversations might be seen as abrupt and unruly in the non-AD/HD world. Here it might be a sign of interest and friendship.

In short, between the AD/HD and non-AD/HD worlds, there is a gulf of communication and understanding that adults with AD/HD often find difficult and frustrating to bridge. People with AD/HD act, think, talk, and process information differently from those without AD/HD. The question becomes how to bridge these two worlds and use your differences to your advantage.

Making a Difference

For adults who have grown up with the experience of being different, their core vulnerability and their greatest hurts have resulted from feeling different. You want to take the risk to stand out—to be heard, to be seen, to be known. But there's also your greatest fear—that of having your differences exposed, which has often brought you humiliation or failure. It is painful to contemplate being seen as different since you've spent your whole life hiding your differences or have been ridiculed for them.

Mixed Messages About Being Different

In our culture, we often disparage those people who go against the tide or who don't hide their differences—unless or until they are successful. Then we idolize them or reward them financially for being so special. On the one hand, we are bombarded with messages to conform and to hide our differences; on the other hand, we are given the message to stand out and be noticed for our individual abilities. No wonder this issue is so loaded for adults with AD/HD!

Ironically, though, it's those very differences, if you put them to work for yourself, that give you the best chance at satisfaction and success. It is in that arena that you may make a unique contribution, where you may be able to express or create something special that is especially your own.

In my book Women with Attention Deficit Disorder, I said to "embrace your disorganization." Now I am telling you to embrace your differences. I know it's very difficult to contemplate this risk of exposure, but at some point in your personal growth, the alternative becomes too painful; consider the emotional consequences of continuing through your entire life without being seen and known for who you are. In Journey One you can take the first step toward embracing your differences by observing how you talk, feel, and what you do about your differences. You can also look at the extent to which you are hiding your differences from other people and the effect this is having on your relationships. (See "Explorations" at the end of this chapter.)

Living with AD/HD every minute and every day is hard work. It is a full-time job, along with whatever else is in your life. The treatment must not also be a life sentence of drudgery and constant vigilance and effort toward turning yourself inside out to become someone else—or, as one client put it, to get over this "terminal case of uniqueness." You and your family members, coaches, counselors, and other professional helpers must not hold out ordinariness, normalcy, or conformity as the litmus test of successful treatment. Aim to appreciate and enhance your differences, instead of defending against them or hiding them.

Remember, no one ever did anything worthwhile by thinking, "What can I do today that won't make a difference?" The good news is that as an adult with AD/HD, you have a huge head start. You are one of a kind. You don't fit in perfectly. You're ahead in the area of differences; now you just have to figure out how to make your differences count. I believe it is in this inability to become like everyone else that those with AD/HD have a chance to use these differences in ways that make them special, with something of value to offer the world.

In his book *The Mind's Eye*, Thomas West says that when people with gifts and learning difficulties or differences succeed, it is not because they have been able to compensate; but instead, their greatness comes from the areas in which they have not been able to compensate. It is not that they have success in doing or saying something special in spite of their difficulties, or because of the strength of character they have had to develop as a result of their difficulties, but rather it is in those areas that are unique that they retain their specialness and extraordinariness.

Explorations

Take the following quiz to assess how you react when confronted with your differences. Periodically take the quiz again to check your progress in this critical area. Mental health professionals can discuss these questions with their clients.

Circle reactions to your differences that you recognize in yourself.

1. How do you talk about your needs or differences?

- **I don't talk about them.**

- **I hide them.**

- **I apologize.**

- **I lie.**

- **I withdraw.**

- **I put myself down.**

- **I overexplain.**

- **I try and convince people that I do have difficulties.**

- **I [put in own words]**

  _____

2. How do you move away from relationships as a result of your differences?

- **I often avoid or withdraw from people whom I feel I have disappointed.**

- I avoid potentially embarrassing people or situations entirely.

- I neglect and hide my differences. I pretend I don't have them. I feel insincere and disconnect; as a result, I don't get close to people.

- I [put in own words]

  _____

3. What thoughts run through your mind (self-talk) when you're asked to do something that doesn't work for you (as a result of your difficulties or differences)?

- How can I say no to more work? If I set limits, my colleagues will think I can't cut it.

- How can I say no to requests for causes I support? I must be very selfish.

- I [put in own words]

  _____

4. What is your self-talk when encountering toxic help (help that is given with a good dose of criticism)?

- How can I ask for anything more in a relationship when I am already such a burden?

- How can I be hurt or angry at my partner/parent/friend when she/he already has helped me so much?

- I [put in own words]

  _____

2

Roadblocks
After Initial Treatment

YOU MAY BE ONE of the first-generation "ADDults" diagnosed over the past several years. This diagnosis most likely brought you enormous relief and hope, even if mixed at times with feelings of grief and loss. Your diagnosis may have been the end of a "Crisis of Confusion," a long search for answers about an array of confusing, baffling, and very troublesome symptoms that you struggled with your entire life. If you are like many adults who weren't diagnosed as a child, the pervasiveness and seriousness of these kinds of struggles may have been invisible to all except those closest to you. Eventually, you may have taken a battery of tests that confirmed the difficulties that you and others may have written off as character flaws.

Finally, after many years, you understood why you felt so different all your life. You knew why so many things never made any sense to you, or why you had so much trouble in some areas even if you did well in others. You began to understand why your life course had led to dead ends and frustration, despite your ability, interest, and early promise.

After this startling discovery and diagnosis, you may have started treatment that probably consisted of education about AD/HD, as well as medication that brought you relief from the most troublesome symptoms. You suddenly could focus, you had energy, and you agreed with the people who said getting treatment was like putting on glasses for the first time. Things began to look up for you, and you let yourself begin to hope again. You may have felt that finally your problems were solved, that everything would now be OK. During this initial period of treatment, you may have received counseling and gone through what we call a "grief cycle" (see chapter 1), where you mourned your losses, felt anger at lost opportunities, and eventually came to what we call "acceptance" of your AD/HD. You may have attended conferences, where for the first time you met other adults like you—a whole new world of people—and realized you weren't alone. This experience was exhilarating, comforting, and educational; you may have seen dazzling slides of brain images and become somewhat of an expert on neurotransmitters. Many of you went home determined to begin your new life. Just think, a new you! This time you could do it!

Your treatment may have ended then, except for periodic medication checks. Or it may have continued with the focus now on getting your life organized. You may have put new strategies in place, using timers, beepers, and planners. You may have gone to support groups where you heard others share their stories of their miraculous cures through medication.

After a while, though, you probably started to notice that even with these newly found tools and information, you began to hit some unexpected bumps in the road. You may have found it wasn't always easy to employ the strategies suggested or to ask for accommodations or help. You may have found yourself, once again, feeling as if you were disappointing important people in your life. Your family and friends sometimes may have seemed perplexed and frustrated when, after this long search and expensive treatment, you still had difficulties. Others didn't believe the AD/HD diagnosis in the first place, dismissing it as a made-up ex cuse. Sometimes you yourself began to doubt the whole thing and became discouraged or disappointed. Or you may have started to think that if you just worked harder and longer, maybe things would change. So you frantically tried one organizational system after another. Or you tried to use the fuel of medication to push yourself even harder. You focused so much on "getting it together" that you followed your routines and schedules even when they were devoid of meaning or excitement.

Don't Mistake Journey One for the Whole Voyage

At a recent first session of a group of adults with AD/HD, we went around the circle for members to introduce them-

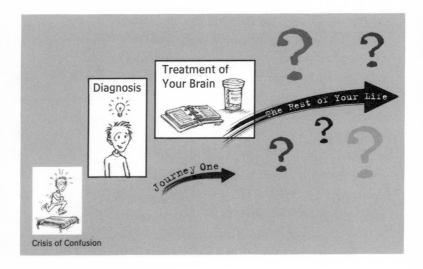

Crisis of Confusion

> The life changes you will undergo as a result of an AD/HD diagnosis are monumental. It will take years, not months, to integrate all the new information and make the needed changes in your life. The emotional upheaval that accompanies this work comes in waves, rather than being a once and forever event.
>
> —Kate Kelly, Peggy Ramundo, and D. Steven Ledingham,
> *The ADDed Dimension*

selves. The newly diagnosed people were dismayed and discouraged to hear many of the members say they had been diagnosed for over five years but were still struggling with many of the same issues.

Many people diagnosed during the "first wave" of adult AD/HD—pioneers, really—have gone underground, only to resurface months and years later still looking for "the answer." If the same professional who initially saw them were to see them again a year or two later, she might hear a completely different story—one of discouragement that things hadn't turned out as they had expected. This feeling of discouragement might arise even when treatment for primary symptoms had been successful!

Some, of course, have been lucky or persistent and have stumbled upon a variety of resources—from coaching to on-line relationships to conferences—that have helped them change their self-image by identifying with other adults who have AD/HD. Unfortunately, many people after the initial AD/HD diagnosis and treatment haven't found that path for themselves and may have gotten stuck.

It is important to know that it is not uncommon to go through a long period of confusion, disappointment, and frustration when the long-term success you counted on doesn't materialize. Treatment often fails not because it's bad but because it stops short after providing effective care for the brain. After so many years identifying so closely with your AD/HD symptoms, you cannot expect your self-image to be instantly corrected with this first part of treatment. Diagnosis and medication alone can't undo all the years of viewing one's self through an incomplete and distorted lens. It can't take away the false expectations, negative beliefs about one's self, and the devaluing view of one's differences. That will take longer.

Beth's Early Experiences with AD/HD

Beth's journeys through AD/HD, which we will follow throughout this book, are representative of a path followed by many adults who have a rocky road to diagnosis and have had a hit-or-miss approach to treatment. Like many adults with AD/HD, Beth is more inattentive than hyperactive. She is sometimes slow in processing information, has difficulty with organization, and is very easily distracted and overwhelmed. She has great trouble getting started on projects and finishing them once she starts. She is also creative, warm, and funny.

How do these types of differences cause pain in the lives of undiagnosed individuals as they grow into adults? Why is it so difficult in certain cases to get diagnosed? One of the reasons is that many adults who are inattentive and not hyperactive may have fallen through the cracks because as children they had structure and support in their lives. Or because they had other protective factors, such as a high IQ or other talents, which shielded them from seeing their difficulties. In these cases, they often don't "hit the wall" until later, after graduating from high school, getting married, or going to college or work. For Beth, who was aware of her differences from the time she was a young girl, the support of her family enabled her to "get by" until she went away to college. Then her life started falling apart.

"CRISIS OF CONFUSION"

Beth's early problems with organization earned her the nickname "Messy Bethie." Although Beth's parents and friends considered this nickname a term of affection, it was not easy to be Messy Bethie. It took young Beth all morning, sometimes all day, to clean up her room, which her mother often made her do before she could go out and begin her Saturdays. In junior high and high school, it took her all afternoon, sometimes stretching into late evenings, to complete her schoolwork. She often brought the wrong folders to class and sometimes even went to the wrong classrooms or to the right classrooms but at the wrong time.

On the other hand, Beth was very creative, and talented in many ways. She loved to express herself—not so much in words, but through dancing and drawing. She and her friends in elementary school used to listen to music and dance for hours. Beth also would make up posters to advertise the school dances and plan the programs and costumes. Because of these talents, Beth's parents and teachers tended to think that her academic difficulties were due to the fact that she wasn't trying or that she had no interest in certain subjects. Still, Beth was smart and somehow managed to get by with C's in math. She liked to make up stories, but she struggled with her English papers since she couldn't figure out how to make outlines or reports in the way her teachers wanted them. Beth would ask the teachers if she could draw the stories instead of writing reports, and she made beautiful displays and sets for stories, often turning them into dramatizations.

Beth had a strong support system—her parents and older sisters helped her a great deal. Her mother would go through her backpack every night and straighten it out and write down the assignments. Her older sisters would sit with her for hours, helping her write the reports. When she was in high school, they would keep her awake the night before exams to study. They would help her type her papers.

Over the years, one of the cornerstones of Beth's identity became her messiness. Naturally, Beth had many other components to her identity. She was talented in art and spent long afternoons as a girl constructing collages from photographs she cut out of her mother's fashion magazines. She was also praised for her ability to put colors together in surprising ways and, in her senior year of high school, won a poster design contest; her award was a free trip to Chicago, where she and the other winners visited the city's art museum. She also got to work as a summer intern in an advertising agency.

Beth had always thought of herself as happy and secure. She looked forward to college, thinking she would have a good time and do well.

But when she went away to college, she lost her support at the same time that the demands on her increased. She had a rude awakening. The extent of her difficulties really shocked her and left her feeling disoriented for a long time. She started questioning whether she really was as responsible and mature as she had always thought. She felt alone and afraid and unable to describe to anyone what was happening to her—the confusion, the fragmentation, the inability to pull things together, the overwhelming disarray all around her. She couldn't find books or clothes or anything else. She couldn't get to class. She frequently couldn't make herself get out of bed. It was all just too much for her—she was too tired.

Finally, one afternoon the resident assistant in her dorm saw Beth crying in her room and tried to be of help. She recommended that Beth talk to someone at the counseling center because many people at college feel this way when they're away from home for the first time; predictably, that's what the counselor thought with Beth. Beth felt a little better now that she had someone to talk to. She cut out all free time and fun and managed to make it through freshman year. She did very well in her art classes.

In her second year Beth shared an apartment with a couple of girls. If she thought it was tough in a dorm, the apartment was completely overwhelming. She was supposed to cook once a week, shop once every other week, figure out bills, keep things orderly. Her roommates were upset with her all the time and called her a "slob," which humiliated her. This sent her right back to the painful feelings of those "Messy Bethie" days. In addition, she was falling behind in her classes and getting depressed. She wasn't talking to her teachers about the problems she was having in school because she already felt so inadequate, she couldn't stand the thought of actually bringing that fact to their attention.

Near the end of the spring semester Beth wasn't able to complete the final research paper for her history class. She had notes all over the apartment, and she couldn't remember what material came from which resources in order to footnote them properly. Instead of asking for an incomplete, she let herself fail the course because it was "too much to deal with." At the same time, her English literature instructor wondered, because of the kinds of problems Beth was having with her papers, if she might have an undetected learning disability. He gave Beth a pamphlet to read on the subject.

That summer, after she failed history, her parents insisted that Beth see a psychiatrist. She was diagnosed with depression and began taking antidepressants. The medication helped her mood a great deal. She began to read some of the books discussed in that pamphlet her teacher had given her. She also had time in the summer to surf the Internet for more information about learning problems. Some of the problems sounded just like hers. She became excited. She decided this would be a good summer to try and figure out what was happening to her at school, so she could fix it before school started again.

Journey One Begins for Beth

Beth went to a psychologist, got tested, and was diagnosed with AD/HD. She really hadn't heard much about AD/HD in people her age. She had thought it was just for hyperactive little boys. This diagnosis scared her because she secretly thought it meant she was stupid. The psychologist taught her some organization and time-management tips, and recommended that Beth ask her teachers for more time on her tests and for turning in assignments. Beth did not want to do this, feeling that having special privileges would be like cheating. In addition, she thought they would think less of her.

When she saw the psychiatrist again after her diagnosis, he prescribed the medication Ritalin. He told her it would

Beth's Schedule

Weekdays

> 7 A.M.: Get up, meditate, eat healthy breakfast, clean up
> 8–10 A.M.: Attend class
> (she chose an early class to learn responsibility)
> 10 A.M.–12 P.M.: Study
> 12–1 P.M.: Get lunch
> 1–3 P.M.: Attend class
> 3–5 p.m.: Study
> 5–6 P.M.: Work out at gym
> 6–6:30 P.M.: Eat dinner
> 6:30 P.M.: Do dishes
> 7–10 P.M.: Study
> 10 P.M.: Clean room and desk; get stuff ready for tomorrow
> 11 P.M.: Go to bed

Saturdays

> Buy groceries
> House-clean thoroughly
> Pay bills the second Saturday of the month

Sundays

> Do laundry at laundromat
> File papers, straighten clutter

Resolution

> *I will not do anything else until these chores are all done. Only then can I go out with friends.*

help her at school. After a few visits in which he made sure she didn't have side effects, he told her that he would see her in four months. And off she went, back to school, hopeful again.

During Beth's junior year, she lived alone so she would

have less to "deal" with—less stress, she thought. Sure enough, there was less stress, but there was also no stimulation or structure. The Ritalin seemed to work pretty well, and she felt she was doing much better—so much so that she decided not to ask the teachers for the recommended accommodations. She wanted to try to get along on her own first to prove she was smart enough, and not use AD/HD as an excuse. She tried harder. She worked harder as well, which was possible due to the medication. Now that she was being treated with stimulants and had strategies to become more organized and disciplined, Beth set out on what she believed would be the beginning of a new clutterless life, as well as a new era of success in school.

Beth drew up a rigid schedule for herself, posting it on her mirror in the bathroom, in the kitchen, and on the front of her day planner.

Beth followed her new schedule for only a couple of days before starting to feel depleted. She became even more disorganized, isolated, and depressed when she couldn't keep to this schedule. She began to forget to take her medication. She stopped going to her 8 A.M. class. By the end of the fall semester, she had failed two classes and was always exhausted.

Beth began to wonder what the point of all this was. It didn't matter that she had so-called talent in art. She wasn't amounting to anything! It was difficult for her to value her talent, she thought, since it wasn't helping her to pass these courses. Beth began to see herself as a loser. She thought her parents must be even more disappointed now that she had been diagnosed and treated and still was not doing very well. This very bright young woman started to think that maybe she just wasn't cut out for college.

It wasn't that making and trying to keep to a schedule was a bad idea; of course, it's helpful for a person with AD/HD to have a structure and a schedule in order to function well. But problems can develop when one goes overboard in an effort to control oneself, and then the tool becomes self-defeating and demoralizing. The rigidity becomes oppressive. In addition, treating oneself like a critical taskmaster is often a setup for failure.

Beth dropped out of school after the first semester junior year. She moved back home. Her parents couldn't understand what had happened because they had gone through so much to get her diagnosed and on medication. How could this be? Though we often speak of someone hitting a wall before diagnosis and treatment, it also is very common for adults to hit a wall sometime after diagnosis and treatment.

Beth "Accepts" Her AD/HD

Beth took the second semester off and began to rethink her life in this new context. She started counseling with a professional who knew about AD/HD in adults. For the first time, she started to understand the bigger picture. The counselor explained AD/HD and life with AD/HD to her in a way she could absorb and understand. The focus of her work with this person was not exclusively on medication, or even on her problems, but instead on Beth as a person: her inner experience, her life, her dreams, her goals, her challenges. In other words, the counselor and Beth began to fill out the full picture of who she really was. With support, and after reading many of the books on AD/HD, Beth decided to go to the local community college and take a few courses that she needed for an associate degree. The counselor gave her the name of a tutor who could help her write papers and recommended a professional organizer for her room at home. Unfortunately, Beth was too embarrassed to call the tutor or the organizer; her mother helped instead. The counselor gave her the numbers of a few support groups. But she didn't go to meetings, because now that she was on medication, was at home, and had less pressure and less to take care of, she started to feel pretty good.

As a result of the good treatment she was receiving, Beth was able to be more focused. She had more energy and was able to take more action. She bought new planners, heard the speakers at AD/HD conferences, and learned all about neurotransmitters. She again felt much more hopeful that she "wouldn't let this AD/HD stop her." She began to understand that AD/HD wasn't about her character or her intelligence. Although she wished she had identified her problem earlier, and shed some tears over all the time she had lost, she reached the point where she could say, "I accept my AD/HD." Now she wanted "to get moving and get over it!" She worked hard with this counselor to move out on her own and prove to her parents that she was responsible after all. She was able to get a job in an office as a secretary to support herself.

The Honeymoon Is Over

The first time I met Beth was four years and many secretarial jobs later, when the honeymoon was over—in spite of getting good treatment for her primary symptoms. She was at a place where she couldn't move forward unless she had some more counseling or worked on the psychology of having AD/HD. She had the distorted notion that "if I just try harder, I can conquer this. I don't want to be like this. I

want to be normal." She was still asking herself, "Why am I still disorganized?"

Beth hit this roadblock because she had false ideas about herself and false expectations about the destination of her travels.

False Expectations and Pseudo-Acceptance

Many people get stuck at this point in their AD/HD experience because they don't want to hear that the goal is not to "get over it" but to "get on with it"—to get on with their lives. Instead, they want to try harder, hoping that sheer willpower will pull them through.

These individuals focus all their efforts on getting over this part of themselves that they hate. Even though they say they have accepted their AD/HD, it is a false acceptance, or a pseudo-acceptance. Many feel like failures months after their initial period of hope and relief; they become resigned to giving up their dreams. Others wind up depleted from redoubling their efforts, using the fuel of medication to work even harder to try and catch up.

If you are stuck in Journey One because of false ideas about yourself or false expectations, you may recognize in the following descriptions your own patterns of fears or blocks that are keeping you from being yourself.

- *Mea culpa.* **You keep working off some perceived debt—either to your family or God or someone you've offended. You feel you should be permanently punished and absorb blame for whatever goes wrong.**

- *Death by normality.* **You are saying or doing all the right things, making all the right commitments, sticking to your schedules, and doing all the things you believe will make you seem "normal" or non-AD/HD. However, you feel disengaged from your true purpose or authentic sense of self. This can result in either tremendous feelings of despair or "nonfeeling," of emptiness inside—what I call "death by normality."**

- *The Shawshank Effect.* **After many years of searching and then finally being diagnosed, you feel a freedom as great as if you were just let out of prison. But now you have no idea how to live or who you are in this new world.**

- *The Pygmalion Effect.* **This effect occurs**

when, after the initial exhilaration of diagnosis, you begin to taste the first fruits of success. It is at this point that treatment usually ends. However, because your new identity has not yet been solidified, you don't know how to successfully and consistently operate in this new world. You are then suspended between the two worlds of pre- and postdiagnosis, in a sort of limbo.

- *Sisyphus.* Like Sisyphus, you are condemned every day to roll the same heavy stone up a huge mountain. You keep making the wrong choices or taking too much. You fail to enjoy your strengths or abilities because you are intent on being "fixed."

- *Fear of shining.* Because of your past difficulties, you now have a "fear of shining." You want to succeed, but you are afraid to try again. So you limit how far you will let yourself go. You are afraid of getting burned again by your dreams if you fly too high. You remember the myth of Icarus, who fell to his death when one of his wings melted as he flew too close to the sun. You may even fear that you won't get off the ground and will be humiliated for trying.

- *Pandora's box.* You try desperately to hide the real you, choosing to remain unfulfilled rather than let others know who you are. Your authentic self stays

It is important to know that if you still feel discouraged, overwhelmed, resigned, or frustrated—despite successful treatment for your primary symptoms—you haven't failed. This is just an indication that your search or your treatment needs to shift from an exclusive focus on the primary symptoms of AD/HD to address the issues of pain, yearning, and longing for meaning and authenticity. You may be looking for the wrong signs or markers and putting your new energies into the wrong places. Even though you have been given tools, you may feel lost and stranded, floundering in this "brave new world" that treatment has handed you. It takes a long time to understand who you are, now that you've landed in this strange new place.

locked up tight in what you perceive to be Pandora's box. You fear that if you begin to open the box, this will bring you even more painful feelings. You may fear that you will be overwhelmed by memories of past failures or humiliations, so you keep your differences under lock and key.

Moving On

When you hit a roadblock after that honeymoon period, it can be disconcerting. Instead of completely disappearing, primary symptoms continue to present difficulties. Friends and family may begin to see less improvement or even feel that nothing has really changed. You begin to feel that something has gone wrong, and you may even feel afraid that you will regress or have already regressed. This roadblock is a natural part of the journey. It signifies that you are probably at or near the end of Journey One and are ready to move on to new experiences and tasks that focus more on your view of your difficulties than on the symptoms themselves.

In their book *Performance Breakthroughs,* Geraldine Markel and Judith Greenbaum tell a story about Michelangelo, discussing his beautiful statue *David* as a metaphor for understanding the learning-challenged student. When asked to explain how he created such a perfect David, Michelangelo replied, "The perfect David was already in the stone. I just had to chip away at everything that wasn't David."* In the context of AD/HD, this means that the point of treatment for AD/HD is not to create a new person, but to allow you to emerge and become fully who you are. The marker that indicates you're ready to move on to Journey Two, where the focus changes to the self and the view of your differences, is that you have gone as far as you can for now working on your primary symptoms.

It is a huge step to get diagnosed, to take medication, to connect with the world of adult AD/HD, to understand why you have felt different all your life. Now you must go deeper; it will take much longer to come to terms with and learn how to live comfortably with your differences.

* Geraldine Markel and Judith Greenbaum, *Performance Breakthroughs for Adolescents with Learning Disabilities or ADD* (Champagne, Ill.: Research Press, 1996), _____.

Explorations

To explore the deeply ingrained yet unspoken expectations that may be holding you back, answer the following questions:

- **How will you know when you have been successfully treated for AD/HD?**

- **What do you think will change in your life at that point?**

- **How will you be different?**

- **Will you be over your AD/HD?**

- **Will you consider yourself fixed?**

- **Do you hope or expect to be more or less like yourself at that point?**

- **What do others close to you expect?**

- **When will you let yourself move on with your life while continuing to struggle with the AD/HD?**

- **What marker of success are you waiting for before beginning to live your life?**

- **In what way might your "acceptance" really be resignation?**

Crisis of Identity— Focus: Your "Self"

3

Seeing Your
"Self" Clearly

FEW YEARS AGO while I was giving a speech at a large AD/HD conference, the complimentary glass of water gave me some unexpected problems. Every time I took a drink, I would spill a little of the water as I struggled to place the glass on one of the three built-in shelves at the back of the podium while remaining focused on the audience. Although I knew I was spilling the water and having my usual difficulties with attempting to coordinate more than one activity at a time, I had assumed that I was concealing my mess behind the podium quite nicely and was proud of myself for continuing on as though nothing at all had happened. However, when I came out from behind the podium after finishing my speech to answer questions, I saw that all my spilled water had seeped out from below the podium and had been gradually forming a rather noticeable puddle. I stood next to the puddle facing an audience of more than a hundred people.

So there I was in a very public setting, my weaknesses and strengths clearly on display. Had I still been waiting for my AD/HD problems to vanish, I would have been crushed by the awkward incident, clear proof that I had failed to "conquer" my AD/HD. And as I was faced by this proof, I would have seen myself as a complete mess and would have left the hall that evening saying the sort of things to myself that I so often hear my clients saying. *I'm a complete slob. I can't be out in public. I can't let anyone see me this way.* I would have retreated into my "messy" self until I felt that I had mastered the art of smoothly coordinating various activities, and only then—which means perhaps never—would I have come out of hiding. In short, the incident of the spilled water would have wiped away all my sense of accomplishment, and I would have only the difficulties of my AD/HD.

However, since I was at another point in my own voyage through life with AD/HD, I was able to focus on my success. After all, my audience seemed more interested in what I had to say than in the puddle I had made. Certainly, I was somewhat embarrassed. But I did not let a little spilled water wipe me out. Instead, I saw the humor in the situation and said, "That's my personal demonstration of AD/HD for you." Everyone in the audience laughed, and I proceeded to answer their questions. In fact, my remark seemed to give them permission to acknowledge their own foibles and to laugh at themselves.

The Search for Your Real Self

For many adults with AD/HD, it's not so easy to step away from their private messes and public blunders. When these adults look at themselves, they focus mostly on their deficits because over the years they have come to identify and evaluate themselves completely through their AD/HD weaknesses, thereby distorting the way they see themselves.

If you have been seeing yourself through a narrow or distorted lens, you will need to expand or broaden your view and begin to notice not just your deficits but your strengths as well. In this wall, you will start developing a clearer picture of the real you. Noted psychoanalyst Karen Horney defined the real self as the "personal unique center of us that wants to grow." One challenge you face in your treatment is to find your real self—even when it's been hiding behind your AD/HD symptoms for years.

The focus in Journey Two is on this search for self. Once you find your real self, the ultimate goal is to accept it. Just as the successful resolution of the grief cycle (discussed in detail in chapter 1) leads you to accept your diagnosis of AD/HD, in Journey Two you move on to accept *yourself*.

I call this journey the "Crisis of Identity" because trying to forge a new sense of self can be extremely rough. It takes time to accumulate new experiences and to expand your self-view and your view of your past dreams enough to move on to a new vision of the future and integrate it with a new identity. With that new identity comes a new vitality, a new sense of purpose and excitement. Your feelings about your differences will change dramatically: You will be able to value your differences, even to develop them and let others see them. This is what we will explore in the next several chapters.

Your organizing style will also change, so that you can accept the idea of getting support when and where you need it. Because you are less vulnerable, see yourself more clearly, you can let people move closer to you and accept their help without it threatening your sense of self. This assistance helps you organize your life.

In this chapter, we will look at various strategies for identifying your self-distortions and developing a more complete view of yourself. You will examine—and begin to revise—faulty beliefs and false expectations, as well as having new experiences of yourself. The challenge at this point is to let go of certain ideas about yourself and expand other ideas about who you are so that you can start getting an accurate and complete picture of yourself.

A Limited Picture of Yourself—
Caught Between a Chair and a Hard Place

When Beth came to see me she was a young woman in her mid-twenties. The first time I met her, she came into my office with a great deal of energy and sat down in the chair across from me. The session began as first sessions usually do—with one exception. After introducing herself and launching into the story of her AD/HD, she suddenly stopped talking, looked down at her chair, and made an un-usual request: "Would you happen to have another chair, a less comfortable chair?" Beth was sitting in a soft, brown leather chair, which matched my own, and it was indeed quite comfortable. "I don't want to be comfortable," she explained. "I want to concentrate. A little discomfort helps me get to work and stay focused." As it turned out, I had a few folding chairs in a closet down the hall and set one up for Beth, who sat down on it and immediately came to a stiff attention. "That's better," she said, half laughing. "It's silly, I know. But a good hard uncomfortable chair helps."

In fact, Beth's experience with discomfort went far be-yond the chairs she chose to sit in. As we've seen, Beth had spent the four years since graduating from community college going from clerical job to clerical job, five of them in total. She did not leave these positions because they bored her or left her dissatisfied, though. She left them because she had been fired for repeated mistakes and organizational blunders. She had come in to see me because she was discouraged and felt that she had gotten nowhere with her AD/HD since her diagnosis at the age of nineteen. She asked me, "How can I feel good about myself if I can't succeed at a basic entry-level clerical job, the sort of job that I should be able to do?"

You may be wondering: Why would someone like Beth, an adult with AD/HD with serious organizational deficits, as well as a talent for art and design, pursue clerical work with such determination? It seems clear enough that Beth was pursuing the wrong sort of goal, the very goal that would keep her from feeling fulfilled. In short, she was truly sitting in an uncomfortable chair. Why couldn't she see this for herself?

Oddly enough, Beth's experience is not atypical of adults with AD/HD. Many of these adults pursue dead-end goals and, when they don't succeed, are left feeling like failures. But how do they come to place so much value in these dead-end goals in the first place?

The Distorted Image

What makes scenarios like Beth's possible is a distorted sense of self. In many cases, this distorted self-image develops over a lifetime of living undiagnosed with AD/HD. Thus the self-distortion has become deeply ingrained, automatic, and will not simply disappear with diagnosis and standard treatment. To make matters worse, many adults with AD/HD don't realize they have a distorted self-image. What came to characterize Beth's identity were not the talents that she clearly had, but her difficulties. What she saw when she looked at herself were her "messes." Gradually, over years, she had come to distort and limit her sense of who she was.

The Explanatory Voice

What Beth lacked while growing up and what could have made her difficulties less trying is what I call an "explanatory voice." This voice is a calm, reassuring, inner voice that develops as we grow into adults, and it helps us explain our experiences to ourselves so that otherwise confusing experiences can be woven into a cohesive self-concept. Unfortunately, because no one understood that Beth had AD/HD, she and others came to understand and explain her "messiness" as a flaw or a quirk of her personality. Many undiagnosed children with AD/HD are called "dreamy" or "absentminded" or "messy." Since AD/HD often goes undetected, these children grow up confused and have no way of understanding why they are different from other children. For this reason, they are unable to integrate an understanding of their differences into a positive identity.

A few years ago, I learned just how important a clear explanatory voice can be to a child when a close friend of mine gave birth to a baby girl who was deaf. Despite her impairment, Lisa grew up to be a perfectly happy and healthy little girl. I have numerous memories of Lisa chatting animatedly with her friends, expressively signing, and apparently feeling not the slightest bit "disabled." Of course, Lisa's deafness was detected from the beginning, and woven into the fabric of her everyday life so that by the time she was a teenager her explanatory voice helped her navigate in the world. For this reason, she was able to develop her strengths and talents, dancing in an after-school perform-ance group and competing on her high school swim team.

Let's speculate, however, on what might have become of Lisa in the following scenario: What if Lisa had never been told that she was deaf, and she was left alone to figure out why she seemed to experience the world so differently from other people? What if nobody told her that words came out of people's mouths, and she never, therefore, learned to read lips? What if no one explained that there were ways for her to communicate, and she never learned to sign? Clearly, without explanations, she would be extremely confused and lack the necessary tools to interact with others effectively and to develop her abilities to their fullest.

While AD/HD and deafness are by no means the same, it's easy to imagine how difficult it is to grow up feeling messy, flawed, confused, and disoriented because you are different but no one tells you why and shows you how to deal with your differences. Those who grow up without in-ternalizing such explanations end up with deeply ingrained distortions that can shape their lives and make it very diffi-cult for them to make productive decisions.

The first step in dealing with a distorted self-image is to realize you have one. If you are self-distorting, you will tend to pay too much attention to your deficits and/or place overblown importance on them. However, if you try to hide or deny your deficits and see only your strengths, your self-image is just as distorted.

Focusing on Your Deficits

Imagine that you have a single dark mark on your face and that every time you look in the mirror you focus only on this one slight spot. You study it from every direction and

wonder if it detracts from your overall appearance. You remember when one of your relatives, or perhaps someone you had a crush on as a teenager, made a comment about this little splotch of dark skin, maybe even suggested that you have it removed. So now when you come into contact with other people, the first thing that occurs to you is whether or not they notice your spot; you carefully study their manner, their gaze for any sign that they have sighted it and been repelled by what you have come to see as a blemish. Finally, intent on getting rid of it, you consult scores of plastic surgeons, all of whom inform you that there will be no getting rid of this mark. Over the years, as you struggle to live with it, you see in the mirror what has now to your eye become a colossal spot that obliterates your appreciation for your green eyes, your high cheekbones, your warm smile. To hide, you withdraw from other people; in turn, they begin to see you as unfriendly and eventually reject you. "Aha!" you say to yourself. "I was right. This awful mark I have on my face has driven people away from me!"

Beth also had a difficult time seeing anything but her deficits. In fact, like many adults who distort, she even began to see her strengths as weaknesses because they tended to distract her from her job. One day she complained to me about the fact that she often doodled at her desk rather than focused on her filing problems at work. In fact, however, what Beth had called "doodling" was actually a well-thought-out, new plan for reorganizing the office space at work. In spite of Beth's protests, the woman at the next cubicle, frustrated with the present work-space configuration, showed Beth's doodles to the office manager, who thought this was a very workable solution to a long-standing problem. But even after her plan had been implemented, Beth didn't really see her accomplishment. "The office looks nicer now," she said, "but my files are still a mess and I'm still a hopeless mess."

Exaggerating importance of deficits gives them a moral dimension, causing you to feel shame, guilt, and a sense of personal failure. When adults place overblown importance on deficits, they see their deficits as tantamount to some kind of sin and will judge themselves far too harshly. They even globalize the problems of their AD/HD until they begin to feel that they are "bad" people.

Beth reflected this sort of shame when she said to herself: "How can I feel good about myself when I can't do a simple job that anyone can do? I can't even file a document properly. I'm a terrible person, irresponsible and lazy." She couldn't differentiate between her lack of secretarial skills and her value as a person. Predictably, her failure to be a successful secretary began to poison the rest of her life. After months of making mistakes at work and being reprimanded by her supervisor, she redoubled her efforts and began to spend more and more time at the office.

Eventually, Beth's social life began to fall apart, though not merely due to time constraints. Beth also felt she would be a burden to her friends. "Who would want to be my friend?" she thought to herself. Without a social life to get in the way, Beth began to work even more hours. Exhausted, she made the sort of mistakes that devastated her. At this point, all Beth had was the part of her life—work— that was the least satisfying. She no longer spent time with friends doing everyday activities (such as conversing, dancing, seeing movies) that might replenish her and give her some joy in life. Nor did she have the time or the energy to take up a job search or even think about this possibility. Beth had created the very conditions that would ensure her failure.

Jennifer, a housewife in her late thirties, also exaggerated the importance of her deficits. She felt she had to manage her household, as well as care for her children and her husband, despite her severe problems with attention and organization. When I suggested that she hire a housekeeper or a baby-sitter, she refused. It wasn't that Jennifer lacked the money to hire help. Rather, completing the tasks that were most difficult for her had become the very cornerstone of her value as a person. But, to come close to becoming what she thought of as an ideal mother and wife, she needed to spend all her time at home focused on her projects.

Needless to say, this effort exhausted Jennifer. And the countless hours invested in cooking, cleaning, and organizing did not always guarantee success. Every now and then,

she would forget to pack her children's lunches for school or accidentally leave out a key ingredient in the recipe she was preparing. Because all of Jennifer's time and her entire sense of self-worth were tied to these domestic duties, when such oversights happened she would feel like a complete failure. She would then globalize the difficulties of her AD/HD and see them as a reflection of her moral character. "I'm no good as a mother and wife," she would tell herself. "I am a terrible person, irresponsible and lazy."

Since Jennifer believed that she needed to spend every minute of her time and every ounce of her energy keeping things perfectly organized and running smoothly for her family, the only time she felt she could take for herself was in the late evenings when the children and her husband were in bed. To escape her clutter and the pressure and the sense of failure at home, Jennifer had resorted to spending one night a week at the local bus station, which was a fifteen-minute drive from her house. It was a quiet, relatively safe place where she could spend the hours between eleven at night and six in the morning—the only guilt-free hours she allowed herself.

During those quiet nights at the bus station, with the few employees cleaning up and the handful of travelers waiting for buses, she felt a certain kind of peace. Watching the people and buses, she would dream of places she might go where she could escape her clutter and all her tasks. Maybe on a desert island she would have nothing with which to create clutter, and she would finally be free. Sometimes she would daydream about living in faraway places, maybe helping poor children in a hospital, doing something important.

At the same time, however, Jennifer had created a trap for herself. For when she arrived home the next morning, she was tired and therefore more vulnerable to making the sort of mistakes that would crush her and leave her demoralized once again.

Focusing on Your Strengths

Unlike Jennifer and Beth, who can see only their difficulties, many adults with AD/HD are able, even before diagnosis, to focus on their strengths. These individuals tend to be gifted or talented in some way and learn early on that they are praised and appreciated for their strengths and derided for their weaknesses. As a result, they make every effort to hide or deny their deficits while enjoying the praise they get for their talents. But because they fail to see and work with their deficits, they end up making poor decisions and running themselves down just as much as those who can focus only on their deficits.

Lance, whose one-man public relations firm took up all his time, is such a person. From childhood, Lance was praised for his intelligence, quickness, and creativity. He excelled in nearly every subject at school and pursued more extracurricular activities than most students. Despite his unexplained problems with organization, punctuality, and limiting his workload, his parents came to expect him to earn straight A's in school, which he did even if this meant he had to work late into the nights and over weekends. In a sense, Lance was good at working unreasonably long hours and at multitasking because his type of AD/HD makes him

seek out high levels of stimulation. What for others is un-
bearable stress is for Lance and adults like him thrilling,
even necessary if they are to focus on and remain interested
in activities.

Unfortunately, always juggling too many projects and activities at once periodically caused major problems for Lance
during his high school years. Usually he was able to get by
with his charming personality and considerable talents, but
on several occasions that still haunt him Lance's precarious
number of projects would crash down around him.

He remembers a time when he was studying for finals,
playing football, managing his best friend's campaign for
class president, and acting in a school play. Lance was in over
his head. He slept through his finals because he had stayed
up all night working on an overdue class project. He missed
a key football game simply because he had forgotten when
the game was scheduled. His friend lost the election because the flyers never got out in time for the campaign, and
his friend never forgave him. As a consequence of all this
stress, he forgot several key lines during the school play.

This experience served to make him even more determined to hide and deny his deficits. The idea that he was
doing something wrong was too much for Lance to deal
with. He began blaming others. He blamed the stupid alarm
clock, he blamed the teachers for not appreciating creativity, he blamed the stage manager for not prompting him
well, and he blamed his friend for feeling angry with him
when Lance had done so much work for him.

Ironically, he began to develop a negative self-view despite the fact that he could see only his strengths. Because
he would deny his difficulties, and felt too vulnerable to get
support, he continued to make mistakes that ultimately dis-

appointed people, the very thing he was trying to avoid. Because he needed and enjoyed high levels of stimulation, Lance was unable to balance his life; he lived constantly on the verge of a crash. Until he accepted that his deficits affected him greatly and that he needed to get help for them in order to continue to use his strengths in a way he could feel good about, Lance would not be able to alter his cycles of activity that led to his periodic crashes. It wasn't his primary AD/HD symptoms alone that were causing all these problems; it was his denial of the problems and his perception of his difficulties that prevented him from filling in his gaps, from getting guidance in making realistic choices.

His counterproductive coping strategies followed him into adulthood and took their toll. Lance was well respected for his excellent public relations work; his clients overlooked the fact that he was often late with his projects because they saw that he was one of the best in the business. But his home office was a perpetual mess. (In fact, Lance was glad he worked from his home. All appointments with his customers were conducted off the premises so they wouldn't see the disarray of his work space.) He spent all his time at his computer and kept six or seven projects going at one time. He could hardly ever stop himself from taking on more work, thinking up new projects, and performing many tasks simultaneously even if this often meant he was frequently on the edge of disaster. While Lance usually delivered for his clients, he was unable to do much for himself or his family. He often forgot to bill his clients, and with many of his projects he had a difficult time determining how many hours to bill for because it took him so much longer to complete the job than it would the average person.

Now and then, Lance tried to get some office help. But since he would not face his difficulties in many areas of management, he was unable to communicate his needs very well. In addition, Lance continued his longtime habit of blaming others for the problems that arose, since he could not see how he was often the source of the problem. After a while, secretaries, accountants, and other assistants found it too hard and chaotic to work with him. He simply would not slow down and allocate tasks in an effective way. Eventually, Lance's wife, who had complained for years that he never had time for his family, left him. Soon after that, he was audited by the IRS. As his disasters accumulated, and at the insistence of his trusted friend and accountant, Lance finally came in to see me.

The great irony of Lance's situation was that he could have been so much more effective in his business as well as his personal life if he had allowed others to support him where and when he needed it. What Lance had to understand and accept before he would be ready to effectively use support, though, was that others would accept him regardless of his deficits, that they would continue to recognize his talents, and, most important, that he might actually be able to sustain their respect and trust by getting support for his difficulties.

The challenge for him when he begins to move toward real acceptance will be to see that his weaknesses do not cancel out his strengths, as he came to believe while growing up. His position is similar to that of Beth and Jennifer, even though the latter tend to see only their deficits. Both types are consumed with fear of deficits: One blocks them out, the other focuses exclusively on them; each strategy has the same effect of distorting reality and causing the person to stay blocked from making informed choices. In Lance's case, he didn't so much hide his deficits as deny them—and push through on talent and personality.

Correcting False Beliefs
by Escaping Negative Feedback Loops

Once you begin to see that you are self-distorting and begin to examine some of your false beliefs, you will need to start the long process of changing these beliefs. You will not be able to expand your sense of self unless you collect new data about who you might be; and in order to collect new data, you need to have new experiences of yourself. Over time, these experiences will be internalized, and you'll develop a new voice that will support you in making good decisions and perpetuate a positive self-image, moving you closer to truly accepting yourself.

This process is a gradual and challenging one. It can also be difficult to begin due to what I call the negative feedback loop, which is often generated by self-distortion and false, incomplete data. When one acts on false information, it can set up a chain of failures that generates more poor decisions and reinforces negative self-views. In *A Comprehensive Guide to Attention Deficit Disorder in Adults,* edited by Kathleen Nadeau, psychologist Kevin Murphy writes about the "importance of recognizing and counteracting the often crippling damage to self esteem that has occurred for many adults with ADD whose condition remained undiagnosed and untreated into adulthood. The cumulative effects of such a history can sometimes lead to internalization of these negative messages . . . many patients become

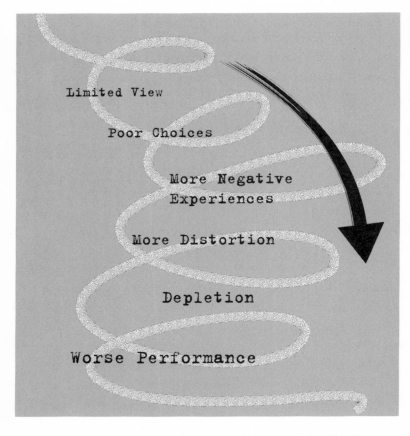

Limited View

Poor Choices

More Negative
Experiences

More Distortion

Depletion

Worse Performance

demoralized over past failures. Helping to rebuild self esteem and self confidence is therefore critical in treatment
of Adult ADD" (p. 137).

Beth, for example, was trapped in a negative feedback
loop. Feeling that she needed to prove herself in a job that
would test her organizational abilities, she became a secretary. When she was fired, she felt as though she had failed
and would need even more desperately to succeed in order
to feel good about herself. Hence her second secretarial job.

The loop pulled her around four times before we began working together to reverse this process. To escape such a loop or even just to begin collecting new data about yourself, you will need to move slowly. Initially, when you begin acting on your strengths and interests, you will not always feel comfortable.

After months of exhaustion, Beth finally decided to take a night out with her friends once a week and go dancing. She had enjoyed dancing on a regular basis a long time ago and so decided to try it out again. On the first night of dancing, Beth felt that she didn't deserve this relaxing experience and could not forget about work, the papers on her desk that needed to be organized, her boss's schedule, a meeting she had to attend the next day. But after a few weeks, Beth began to relax and regain some of the old pleasure she got from a night of dancing. When she came to see me one week, she said enthusiastically, "You know, I really enjoy dancing. I'm good at it, too. I even made small talk. It was really fun. I don't know how long it's been since I've just gone out and had a good time. It's nice to know that I can just relax sometimes." While dancing had nothing to do with Beth's professional life, it became a small outlet of enjoyment for her. It also reminded her that she had strong social skills and that she really loved spending time with people.

This small weekly activity helped Beth begin to reverse the negative process and rebuild a sense of strength and competency. It set in motion a positive feedback loop, which will be explored in the next chapter. Now that she felt better about herself and remembered that she had other gifts and sources of joy, Beth no longer put herself under so much pressure to perform at work. Though she continued to make mistakes, she made fewer ones and no longer felt devastated when her supervisor reprimanded her. More important, now that Beth had begun to see herself more completely, she had taken the first steps toward truly accepting herself.

A New Approach to Organization: Moving Toward Human Support

While we commonly think of organization as managing paper or getting more advanced electronic organizers in order to move along through our AD/HD life voyage, at some point we must move to more internal ways of viewing organization. Throughout Journey Two we will continue to see that by developing a full and accurate self-concept we will be able to increasingly take steps to make our lives work—the actual goal of organizing.

At this point in Journey Two, you make the transition from organizing alone, as in Journey One, to the idea of utilizing support as an effective way to organize your life. By getting adequate support that addresses your difficulties, you can become and remain more physically organized, enabling you to spend more time and energy on what you do well.

Many people who get to this point think of getting support, but sometimes even if they do proceed, the support they seek isn't specific to their difficulties or adequate enough to make a difference. This isn't about typical help, and it isn't a luxury. It's about being able to individualize your needs and view support as assistance you require because of your deficits, and that will allow you to be more productive.

Also, having enough support allows you to be involved with activities that nourish you so that you gain energy to return to these organizational matters. Many adults who get to this point use the reasoning that they simply lack the time to go out and have new experiences. Indeed it does run counter to logic that if you already are short of time you can't cut into that time even more. The truth is, however, that when you make more time by utilizing support, you replenish yourself as well as fill in important gaps. But you may be unable to do this until your whole identity isn't defined by your ability to perform specific tasks well. That is why it is a hallmark of moving along successfully when you find yourself able to admit that you need help and then solicit and accept it.

Jennifer, the housewife who for a long time would not allow herself to leave her "messy" house except when her family was sleeping, felt guilty when she even considered going out during the day to take a little time for herself. Nonetheless, I encouraged her to do it, and when she continued to insist that she simply did not have the time, I encouraged her again to utilize support services.

To be successful in Journey Two, you may need to learn how to use the strengths of others in order to explore your own strengths. This may mean that you need to hire or trade for housecleaners, baby-sitters, professional organizers, coaches, personal assistants, or any one of a number of other resources depending on your particular difficulties. Once you can begin to organize your life around the support you need, you will soon find that you will have not only the time but also the desire and enthusiasm to go out

The Tropical Fish Tank

Even the smallest steps in this process of letting in new data—doing a bit of volunteer work or taking an evening course at a community college—can make a difference. Forming a more accurate self-concept takes place sequentially and by the gradual accumulation of new experiences and data. To illustrate the importance of slow but steady growth, I often use the analogy of the Tropical Fish Tank.

A friend once told me that tropical fish will only grow proportionally to the size of their tank. As the tank size increases, so does the size of these fish. But the tank size must increase gradually. If such a delicate fish is placed in a tank dramatically larger than its last home, it will drown. If, on the other hand, the tank is not exchanged for a slightly larger one, the fish will not grow at all. The challenge for you now is to achieve a balance: You must keep changing to the next size of tank to keep pace with your growth.

and have new experiences. See the "Recommended Resources" section for information on where to find professional organizers, coaches, and other help.

After Jennifer agreed to utilize support services, she hired a cleaning service. The cleaners came every other week to do the big cleaning jobs, but this proved unhelpful to Jennifer. The day before they arrived, she was a wreck, cleaning up and hiding everything. And although they left her with a sparkling clean home, she found that by the next day it was completely disorganized again.

The AD/HD-related problems that caused Jennifer such distress were about her "stuff" and the maintenance of systems, not about the dust. She hadn't found the kind of support that for her would actually be helpful. You have to determine what is the actual source of the drain of time and energy for you. Lance, for example, might not need a secretary who types great so much as someone who will organize his desk twice a day. Get the kind of help that is tailored to your specific deficits. Your willingness to utilize support in this customized way will come only after you have made some progress in seeing that you are not devaluing yourself by accepting support for your needs.

This proved true for Jennifer, who finally agreed to allow a baby-sitter to watch her children for two hours one afternoon a week while she got out of the house. "What will I do for that long?" Jennifer asked me. Because for years she had taken almost no time for herself in the middle of the day, it was difficult for her to answer this question. I suggested going to a café, a movie, or a bookshop that specialized in travel books. The point, I reminded her, was simply to try something new and go someplace where she felt more like herself.

Jennifer chose to go sit at a café, drink tea, and do something she had not done in years: knit. For the first few weeks, she spent these two-hour retreats in a quiet café worrying about her kids and her "messy" home. In fact, she found herself calling the baby-sitter, who told her that the kids were just fine. But over the weeks as she continued to take this one afternoon a week for herself, she came to enjoy it and even look forward to it. "I sit near a sunny window," she told me one week, "and just think about things. I enjoy the knitting, of course. But I enjoy even more just

Remember that even the slightest move in the right direction or the slightest widening of the lens through which you see yourself will keep you on track as you move along in your travels.

getting out and having some quiet time. In the middle of the day when there are actually other people around. I'd forgotten what that's like."

As Jennifer began to escape her negative feedback loop, she began to see herself in a larger context and no longer based her self-worth exclusively on her performance as a housewife. Now that she had some time to herself during the week, she no longer felt the need to spend sleepless nights in the bus station. Better rested, Jennifer made fewer mistakes at home. But even when she forgot to buy the mustard or the cabbage for dinner, it was less of a catastrophe because a little less of Jennifer's identity was at stake. She was beginning to see and think of herself as more than a woman struggling with AD/HD.

After her experience at the café, she was more willing to explore her situation. She saw that she needed to develop the other sides of her identity. Now more willing to seek out help with the house, she hired a college student to come in after school and help her with preparing dinner, a task particularly difficult for her.

A word of warning: While this process may sound easy, it is often a real challenge for adults with AD/HD, many of whom will resist getting the support they need. Resistance may come from feelings of shame and the idea that you must go it alone. When Jennifer expressed these sentiments to me, I urged her to try using a support service for a couple of weeks and see how it felt. I told her to take the leap of faith since she just couldn't believe it. Once she had done that and was able to set up even a subtle positive feedback loop, she saw how learning to use the support of others was a skill and a strength rather than a source of shame.

Beware the Roadblock of Negative Expectations

One more difficulty that anyone who sets out to correct her self-image should look out for is the reflex action of *negative expectations*. After years of making decisions with faulty data and living in sometimes damaging negative feedback loops, many adults understandably come to expect negative outcomes. Those with difficult experiences in their past may be wary of taking the risk and may at times misinterpret certain scenarios and situations in a negative light.

After years of being reprimanded for small organizational blunders that happened as the result of my AD/HD, I still sometimes misread or misinterpret messages in a negative way. Recently, while my secretary and I were working over a weekend to get a last-minute project completed, I was mortified to read in a fax she had just sent to my home from the office, "I *resent* these pages." After I had recovered enough to look more carefully at her message, I saw that she had in fact written, "I *re-sent* these pages." I had initially misread the fax because for years I was told that my writing was cluttered and too difficult to read.

The best defense against these reflexes is to know what they are and what triggers them. Be prepared for those times when the shadow of negative past experiences will fall. Program your developing explanatory voice to recognize a negative reflex when it occurs, explain it to yourself, and see it clearly for what it is. While you may still feel the sting of the past in some present experiences, you will also be able to identify and understand these feelings so that they won't paralyze you.

Your New Expanded Sense of Self

As you proceed on your voyage, it is important at each point along the way to remind yourself of your goals and to understand why you are doing what you are doing. So let me reiterate that expanding your self-view is not a project you take up merely to feel good about yourself and your AD/HD. The challenge of living with AD/HD and its symptoms is a real one and should not be underestimated. If you are to lead a full, satisfying life, how you view your AD/HD differences and the difficulties caused by them is just as crucial to your continuing success as the medication you take. Both are necessary and neither alone is sufficient for adults, because AD/HD is a neurological *and* a psychological event. How you view your differences will largely determine how you see yourself and others; it will also determine many of your critical life decisions.

It was because Beth had not yet learned to see herself apart from her AD/HD that she had devoted four years of her life to becoming a secretary, a goal clearly based on false expectations and incomplete data. In Journey Two, you need to stop focusing exclusively on your primary AD/HD symptoms and begin to work toward the goal of seeing a self that expands far beyond this too-limited picture.

Finally, the point of Journey Two is to begin to form a realistic picture of your whole self so that you can make good choices based on complete data instead of bad choices based on incomplete or inaccurate data. This picture will include the real extent of your deficits, along with the real quality of your strengths and talents. This is not to deny the difficulty of or the ongoing struggle with AD/HD, but

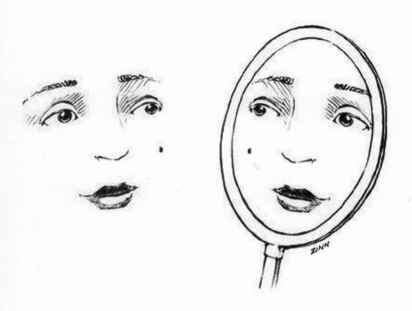

rather to find ways to accept and value yourself as a whole person.

In the next chapter you'll learn how to continue expanding your self-concept through the eyes of others. To see an accurate picture of yourself, you must allow yourself to be reflected by others who can appreciate you and see the whole you. For this to happen, you must learn how to put yourself in situations where you can be seen. Once you have learned to do this, you will be able to let in still more new data as you come to see yourself reflected accurately by others.

At that point, you will move toward true acceptance of your AD/HD, your self, and your differences.

Explorations

Self-Distortion

- **What small blemish in your life are you magnifying?**

- **What strength are you minimizing?**

- **What part of your real self have you lost while focusing on your deficits?**

- **Do you keep having the same negative experience of yourself?**

- **What choices led to this?**

- **What new experiences might you need in order to correct your self-image?**

Identifying Your False Beliefs

The first step toward expanding your self-view is to identify your faulty self-beliefs. Since you may have been distorting for years, you are probably unaware that you are doing this. So it is essential for you to take your time with this section and ask yourself whether any of the scenarios below might describe your life now.

At times, our AD/HD is more noticeable and tends to result in blunders. Our reactions to these blunders can tell us a lot about how we see our AD/HD and may offer obvious clues that we are engaged in one or more of the types of self-distortion discussed in this chapter. For the following scenarios, select the response that fits you the best. Then ask yourself the following questions:

- **How does this belief interfere with my life?**

- **How did I come to believe this?**

- **What would it be like to live without this belief?**

- **What would it take to begin to change this belief?**

- **What barriers would I face in beginning this process?**

- **What can I do to surmount these barriers?**

1. When AD/HD strikes (you have an AD/HD blunder), what do you say to yourself?

- **I am a jerk.**

- **I am so lazy.**

- **I thought I was getting better. Nothing's working.**

- **I am immature.**

2. Wipe Out

Self-distortion makes you believe that others cannot see the good in you or value any of your positive qualities as long as the difficulties of your AD/HD are detectable. Which of the following statements best describes how you feel when others see your blunders?

- **If people have a good opinion of me, it is just because they don't know what I am really like.**

- **If they saw the mess I left behind, they wouldn't have the same good opinion of me.**

- **If I let people get too close to me, I would be "found out" as the impostor I am.**

- **When AD/HD happens, it wipes out for me all sense of worth and accomplishment.**

3. Just Do It

Nike had great success with the advertising slogan *just do it*. However, this approach often leads adults with AD/HD down a fruitless and frustrating path. Too many adults with AD/HD are determined to carry out their counterproductive goals no matter what the cost: If I just do more of what's not working, I'll be able to make it work. If I just work harder, longer, and if I just give up other things that are taking up my time and concentration, things will work. Needless to say, that's a hard wall to bang your head against.

- **I should be able to [fill in the blank] _____, because everyone else can.**

- **If I keep trying to succeed at something,**

but it doesn't work out, I will tell myself to try harder.

- If I berate myself, I will motivate myself. I just need to grow up.

- I spend all my time and energy trying to get organized (my area of weakness).

4. Faulty Equations

The sort of distortion that results from faulty equations is everywhere in American culture. For example, IQ is erroneously equated with school performance and grades with intelligence. By the same token, many adults with AD/HD equate their personal value, their intelligence, their general skill levels with their ability to organize. What these adults need to see is that the difficulties of their AD/HD are separate from their strengths.

- I equate my intelligence or my maturity with my level of organizational ability.

- I equate my intelligence with my school performance.

- I equate my value as a person with my ability to organize.

5. Lowering Sights

If you are making decisions based on faulty equations, you are likely lowering your sights in many of the decisions you make. Again, you need to realize that you can pursue your strengths and talents regardless of your deficits or, if necessary, by seeking help with your AD/HD so that you can focus more on your strengths.

- **If I can't succeed at a job I like because of the organizational demands, it makes sense to get a less challenging position.**

- **I can't even function at home, so I obviously can't succeed anywhere else.**

- **I cut out areas of potential satisfaction in order to control my life instead of moving toward these areas and adding enough support.**

6. *Hiding Out*

If you tend not only to overemphasize your deficits but also to feel ashamed because of them, you will believe you don't deserve help or can't ask for it.

- **Shame causes me to spend countless extra hours searching for some information I have misplaced rather than asking for it again. I don't want anyone to know that I've lost it.**

- **I would rather stay up all night working, or cut out all recreation, in order to present myself well so no one will know about my problems.**

- **I have a hard time admitting I need help with problems related to my AD/HD because to admit this would amount to defeat.**

- **I often avoid or withdraw from the people I feel I have disappointed.**

7. *Gift Wrapping*

Many adults with AD/HD don't see their gifts at all or feel that their gifts are actually getting in their way. As adults learn to stop focusing exclusively on their deficits, they begin to recognize where their strengths lie.

- **I have lost sight of my own abilities and feel cut off from any new possibilities.**

- **I have come to view some of my gifts, such as sensitivity, creativity, and spontaneity, as negatives.**

- **I often don't understand why other people compliment me for qualities that I feel are nuisances and get in my way.**

8. *The Achilles' Heel of Negative Expectations*

Are negative expectations keeping you from taking the necessary risks that will allow you to receive new positive data? Read the messages that follow and then answer the list of questions.

Negative Messages

- **Do you tend to hear any of these negative messages in casual exchanges with others, even and especially when**

**no one intentionally delivered them
to you?**

- **Do you tend to hear such messages as
  reminders of earlier painful experiences
  and so act preemptively by attacking or
  withdrawing?**

- **Do you expect to hear these messages
  often and therefore distort the situation?**

  - **How can you live like this?**

  - **What's the matter with you?**

  - **You fooled us for a little while, but
    we found out the truth.**

  - **You have disappointed us.**

  - **You are too much trouble.**

  - **You are too sensitive.**

Finally, go through the above list again and ask yourself whether any of the responses you checked are clearly the result of former, unpleasant experiences. If so, your negative expectations are getting in your way.

9. The Waiting Game

If you see the process of living with AD/HD as linear, you are putting off the rest of your life until you can finally get organized. As those who play the waiting game know, there's no fun in it. You might just get stuck doing nothing but struggling with your deficits while your strengths and talents go untapped. And if you keep saying the following to yourself, you might never get started with your life at all.

- **I will be acceptable to myself and others when I am fixed or over my AD/HD. Then I will be lovable, mature, acceptable, competent, and worthy of respect.**

- **Everything would be OK if I could just get organized.**

- **I will start thinking about my life when I have some time and space—when everything is under control, everyone's needs are taken care of, and people stop asking me for things.**

4

Reaching True Acceptance

ONE OF THE MOST PAINFUL aspects of living with the differences of AD/HD is being unable to express in a visible and clear way everything you think and know and feel. As a result, many adults with AD/HD often feel invisible; friends, colleagues, and even family members often never really see them. Once you begin to expand your self-concept, it is essential that you begin to cultivate relationships with those individuals who can see adults with AD/HD as whole persons and reflect this more complete picture back to you. They will not merely "accept" your deficits but also truly enjoy you as a complete person. In time these kinds of clear reflections will give you the confidence to take a few more small steps as you begin an extremely important new cycle, continuing to reverse the negative feedback loop.

Don Wears a Cloak of Invisibility

For years, Don was acutely aware that the person whom others saw was not really his authentic self. Instead, they saw a man whose wardrobe was limited, six days out of the week, to gray or navy blue suits, white or light blue button-up Oxfords, and a red or black necktie cinched tightly at his collar. On his feet, Don wore the same brand of black leather dress shoes that he'd worn for the last seven years. He wore these clothes not because he particularly liked them, but because they were worn by most of the men at the large insurance company where he worked as a salesman. Don even drove a certain model of Buick, a car that many of his colleagues drove. When he parked beside a car that resembled his own, when he sat down in his cubicle across from a man who looked similar to him, when his desktop was just as neat and organized as his neighbor's, when his papers were as efficiently arranged and labeled as any of his colleagues' papers, Don felt a temporary comfort in having hidden his differences and having passed for "normal," for non-AD/HD. But his alliance with the "norm" was unholy. He felt at any moment that his cloak of invisibility could slip away, that his charade would be discovered, that he would be found out and his differences exposed.

But while Don was terrified of being seen, he also knew there was another, authentic side of himself that he had locked away and that he longed to share with others. And sometimes Don would slow down when he walked past the front window of the local bookshop and peer in at the new poetry collections, art and photography books, and anthologies of essays and stories.

When Don was finally done struggling with his files at work, he would sit in a comfortable chair at home and remember how, as a child, he had loved having his mother read novels to him. (His favorites were those by Charles Dickens, Robert Louis Stevenson, and Jack London.) On Sundays, after finishing his obligatory reading of the financial section of the newspaper, he eagerly turned to the "Arts" section and might read a review of a new show at the local art gallery or a new exhibition at a nearby museum.

Of course, Don did not go to the gallery or museum or spend much time in bookstores or even take an hour or two to read a chapter of a novel or even a few poems every week. Instead, he spent almost all of his time on his paperwork at the office, arriving at 7:30 A.M. and not leaving again until 9 P.M. Why? Because he had a distorted view of himself. When he looked in the mirror, he saw a man who needed and wanted to succeed in this non–AD/HD world, a man who lived mostly to avoid any reprimands for problems with his paperwork. Don spent all his energy trying (successfully) to keep up with his sales reports and attempting to hide the fact that it was so hard for him to make the kind of small talk that came so easily to the other guys at work.

When Don had his first appointment with me, five years after he had been diagnosed and initially treated for AD/HD, he showed signs of being stuck in the pseudo-acceptance characteristic of Journey One. He wanted me to help him improve his organizational skills at work. He didn't complain that his deeper longings went unrealized or that he wasn't seen for who he really was. No. At first, he was looking for a taskmaster to help him be better at keeping his nose to the grindstone. "I guess," he said, explaining his reason for coming, "I just need you to be tough on me, to make me have more discipline to keep going. I mean, I'm doing well. I haven't caused any problems at work for weeks now, and I want to keep it up."

But Don had dark rings around his eyes. It was clear to me that he was exhausted by the fatiguing and limited life he was struggling to maintain. And over the months that

How to Find People Who See the Real You

Once you have begun to expand your self-view through new experiences of yourself, you will need to develop and understand the criteria by which to choose companions for this important part of your voyage.

Here are some tips to help yourself identify who these people might be and where you might find them.

- **Think about a time when you felt accepted and comfortable in the company of others. Where were you at the time? What were you doing? What was it about these individuals that gave you such a good feeling?**

- **Remember that you will feel relaxed and at your best around people who can see the real you. You won't feel stupid or shy. You will be able to speak easily or feel at ease not speaking at all. In short, you will simply feel good just being yourself.**

followed, I suspected that he had really come in for the sake of that part of himself that wanted to be visible, that longed to be himself again, though Don at this point didn't yet believe there was any hope of this.

Don Begins to Expand His Self-Concept

I began to notice that Don was a hidden lover of the arts when, from time to time, his eyes would light up and his voice would take on a tone of excitement as he spoke about art and music, or about a favorite poem he learned years ago that continued to move him deeply. Over a period of many months, as Don and I worked together, he began the process of expanding his self-concept by attending a few evening lectures in art history at a local community college. As he slowly came to see this side of himself again, his reports at work began gradually to stop dominating his life so completely. He became a little more relaxed and energized. He was beginning to lett in new data (as we discussed in the previous chapter).

To keep expanding his self-view, Don now needed to take the next step: to let himself be seen by others who could help reflect back to him the full and accurate picture of himself. But like many adults with AD/HD, Don had trouble with this step. For years he had put himself in an environment where people saw mainly his deficits and he had come to see himself in the same way. His colleagues at the office saw Don as a clumsy person who would from time to time spill a drink in the cafeteria and oftentimes, during conversations, wander off in unexpected and surprising directions so that he had a reputation for being "absent-minded." This meant that Don would need new people in his life who could not only share his deep interest in literature but also appreciate him fully and see his strengths along with his difficulties.

Bear in mind that you don't always have to make a concerted effort to find people who see and reflect the real you. Once you've begun expanding your view, examining your longings, letting new data in, and shifting your interests and values to better suit your more accurate picture of yourself, you may very well discover that you're associating with these very people.

How to Be Seen Accurately

Adults with AD/HD often have difficulty being seen and recognized for who they are, not merely because they distort and try too hard to fit in. Their AD/HD simply gets in the way. Don, for example, had a hard time articulating his true thoughts and feelings, especially when put on the spot. He often blurted out non sequiturs, or he tended to freeze up during conversations about issues that really mattered to him, though inside he had a torrent of ideas that he would have loved to discuss. He just needed more time. To make matters worse, his many bad experiences with this problem in the past meant that he had negative expectations and put himself under the sort of pressure that makes small successes that much more difficult.

In contrast to Don, Petra, a woman in her mid-forties, came off initially to others as brusque, abrupt, even antagonistic because of her AD/HD. Like many individuals with AD/HD, she tended to move at a faster pace than most people are used to. As a result, she was sometimes impatient, completed other people's sentences, and, in short, was overeager to cut to the chase. People tended to see Petra as rude and inconsiderate, even though deep down she was a funny, sensitive, and caring person. Because people had either not taken the time or hadn't had the opportunity to get to know the real Petra, she had received negative and incomplete reflections for years.

Another reason why Don and Petra failed to be seen accurately for so many years is that they did not spend much time in an environment where people were likely to take the time to know them and appreciate who they really were. As we have seen, Don spent most of his time at work, where his business-minded colleagues did not share his interests. Even when one of his peers would ask for his opinion about a recent movie, Don might say something completely unrelated like "Hot enough for you today?" and would be labeled a "space case." Petra, on the other hand, received cold treatment from others, who kept their distance; some people even told her outright that she was rude and unkind.

If you are like Don or Petra, you may profit from putting yourself in a less risky setting where you can interact with other adults with AD/HD. These individuals are more likely to understand you, see the whole you—including your strengths—and enjoy your company. Fortunately, there are now more venues of support available for adults with AD/HD than ever before. Many adults meet and form relationships in on-line chat rooms. Others get acquainted at weekend seminars or conferences on AD/HD or in the context of AD/HD support groups. Still others enter therapy.

Don Reveals His True Self at a Weekend AD/HD Conference

Because he needed a new and safer environment in which to get started, Don attended a weekend conference for adults with AD/HD, an experience that would dramatically alter his view of himself and his differences. On the first day of the conference, he walked about from seminar to seminar wearing his usual suit and maintaining a safe distance. To his surprise, he discovered that there were hundreds of adults whose past histories rivaled his for twists and turns. Don actually overheard a woman speaking about her own

difficulty with articulating her thoughts. In one discussion group, a man dropped his notebooks and said jokingly, as loose paper floated to the floor, "The good old one-two drop and flutter." Don was surprised by the ease and good humor with which people shared their stories of past mishaps as well as their stories of success. One woman stood up and talked about how, after years of stalling, she had finally decided to begin to write and had managed to publish two articles that year. "All the same, my desktop is still a sea of papers. But at least I'm finally doing the work." This was a first for Don; he was actually seeing people like himself talking honestly and openly about both their difficulties and their very real successes.

The next day, feeling more relaxed, Don put away his suit and wore more casual clothes and carried a book of poems by one of his favorite poets as a way of identifying himself and his interests to others at the conference. At lunch, he found himself at the same table with the woman who had been talking about her publishing successes the day before and who was herself, Don now discovered, a fan of this same poet, whose life and work they discussed over their Greek salads. Don stumbled at first and felt some of his usual nervousness, but noticed that his new discussion partner listened to him patiently and that she also needed time to formulate her thoughts. As he relaxed and settled into the conversation, another side of Don began to emerge. He was now dressed in clothes that felt most comfortable to him and discussing his favorite poems, not talking about premiums, claims, deductions, liabilities, and where in his filing system each of these categories belonged. He was actually reciting some his favorite passages; he even shared a poem he had written a long time ago. Don found himself, for the first time in years, feeling comfortable in his own skin and connected to others in a way that made him feel very much like his true self.

PETRA GETS POSITIVE FEEDBACK
AT A PERSONAL-GROWTH RETREAT

Petra also needed a more controlled and structured environment in which to begin collecting more accurate reflections of her true self. However, not all adults with AD/HD will need to seek out exclusively AD/HD settings. More than anything else, Petra needed a space in which people would get to know her over time. For this reason, she attended a five-day personal-growth retreat, where she could feel safer revealing herself along with her AD/HD difficulties.

During the first days, she noticed the adults in her group backing away from her and acting a little defensive around what they had taken to be her antagonistic behavior. However, after she spent a few days sharing personal stories, as well as eating lunch and dinner, with them, they began to see through Petra's surface to the caring and sensitive woman inside. By the end of the retreat, Petra told her group that they had given her the first positive reflections she could remember receiving.

A Reminder of the Goals of Journey Two

At this point in your journey, as you, like Don and Petra, begin to experience accurate reflections from others, you should remember that the long-range goal of this journey is not the reflections themselves. Nor is it spending time around others with AD/HD. Nor is it spending time at conferences or retreats or in therapy. These are all tools that you may or may not need on your way to the larger goals of this journey: (1) building a more cohesive, accurate self-view which you can internalize and refer to in the future; and (2) accepting and valuing yourself and your differences regardless of whether others see you or not. After all, you cannot always be around others who see all of you at all times. You can't spend every day at an AD/HD conference. But as you begin building a more solid self-view, you will seek out people who share your interests. And you will have the confidence to explore larger and more challenging settings.

You may have family members or friends who see you clearly and fully enough for you to start developing or expanding a new view of yourself without having to put yourself in a special setting. If so, you're one of the lucky ones. What's essential is that you have at least one person in your life who can see the whole you. Once you have that confirmation, you can be around others who may see only parts of you while still effectively working toward your goal of building a new and fuller self-concept.

At this early stage, try to avoid as much as possible the company of those who see *only* your faults unless these people are important to you in some way—family members, old friends, coworkers, and bosses, for example. Such relationships will also tend to shift as you progress in your travels. As more and more people see you accurately, you will begin to respond differently to those who do not, giving off the sort of signals and cues that will allow them to know you value yourself, and they will often respond accordingly. In Journey Three, you will learn to develop and use a variety of communication skills that will make these shifts in relationships much easier. For now, however, you should be careful not to spend a disproportionate amount of time with those who see only your deficits. If for some reason you must do so, you have to offset this experience by spending time with people who can see all of you.

Positive Feedback Loops and Valuing Voice

Once you have even a slightly corrected or expanded self-view, you can use that information to make better, more informed choices that take into account your strengths and deficits. This gives you a better chance at success, and the new successful experiences enhance your image even more, leading to better choices. These positive experiences build on and lead to more positive experiences, creating a positive feedback loop.

Once you begin to be seen and receive good reflections from others, you'll start to internalize and integrate into your self-view the accurate reflections of others, what I call a valuing voice.

The valuing voice is most easily understood in terms of its opposite, the devaluing voice, which most adults who distort

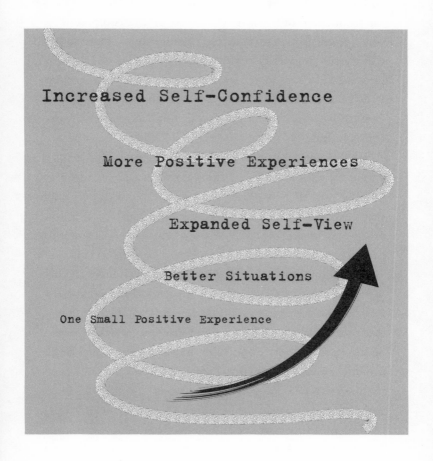

Increased Self-Confidence

More Positive Experiences

Expanded Self-View

Better Situations

One Small Positive Experience

have internalized. The devaluing voice exaggerates the importance of and overemphasizes deficits. It personalizes your difficulties in a critical way. The valuing voice, on the other hand, takes in a larger picture—not only your deficits but your strengths as well. Moreover, it values you as a person apart from your strengths or deficits. And it remains stable.

If you look at yourself in the mirror under the influence of the devaluing voice, you see only the blemish of AD/HD and forget to look at the rest of your features. But after having heard from others who have seen a more complete version of you, you return to the mirror having internalized these reflections and begin to see and value your many pleasing features. Together with your explanatory voice, your valuing voice will help you continue to expand your view of yourself, set up positive feedback loops, and move through Journey Two.

To illustrate this process, let's pick up in Don's story where we left off. After returning from the AD/HD conference, he was able to absorb some of the picture of himself that others had given him. He was now ready to seek out reflections in non-AD/HD settings where he was likely to find people who shared his interests.

One night, Don actually allowed himself to leave the office a little early to participate in a poetry discussion group that met weekly at a local bookstore/café. While sitting in a back corner of the bookstore and listening to what people had to say, Don felt comfortable and intensely interested in the discussion. But when the small group—all strangers to Don—moved to the café and gathered around a table to continue the discussion over coffee, Don felt a small, familiar sting of discomfort. No one else in the group wore a suit and tie or looked anything like him or any of his colleagues at work. Don felt intimidated by a few graying men with round spectacles and small beards who he assumed were much smarter than he. The group leader was a young man with long wavy hair that fell over his shoulders, and Don hoped desperately that this man would not ask his opinion about anything.

At that moment, however, something surprising happened to Don. He recalled his experience at the AD/HD conference where he tended to bond and spend time with individuals who, despite their AD/HD, were as intelligent as this group of non–AD/HD adults. And as the evening progressed and the discussion escalated, Don found himself captivated by what others had to say and so absorbed by the discussion that he began to forget his hesitations. The relaxed and eccentric appearance of the discussion group was refreshing, accustomed as he was to the more formal and conservative appearance of his colleagues at work. Taking off his heavy blazer and loosening his tie, he began to participate in the discussion. At one point he even felt himself commanding the attention of the whole group, who listened with interest and responded well to his particular interpretation of a poem. Without quite noticing it fully at the time, Don was clearly at home and in his element, interacting with people who shared his interests and could appreciate a whole side of himself that others had not seen in many years.

Building Internal Storage Space with the Help of a "Witness"

At this point, when you, like Don, have taken these initial steps and begun to have positive experiences, it will be important to hold on to and store the reflections of those who can truly see you. Just as your outer environment needs more storage spaces to prevent your papers from disappearing into a black hole, your internal environment needs to be arranged to hold and keep data about yourself. Because your old self-image was incomplete and inaccurate, you will begin this process of gathering new and fuller reflections of yourself with an inadequate shelving system, so to speak. Initially, you may have room enough only for your "messy self" or your "clumsy, awkward self," depending, of course, on how you've come to see yourself over the years. But as others begin to see and reflect back to you a wider range of your qualities—your unique sense of humor, your intellectual intensity, your creativity, your spontaneity, and any number of other qualities—you will need to make storage space to hold these reflections.

Without this necessary internal space, it may be very easy for you to let these reflections fall off the shelves. You will know if you are stuck at this point in Journey Two if you fail to see your progress or tend to brush it aside or see it as small and irrelevant. Keep in mind, however, that because this process takes place gradually and by the accumulation of small steps, you'll need to resist the temptation to forget or disregard your forward momentum, no matter how seemingly slight. Those who wait for a large success to come into view might never get started on this process.

You will need one person or a group of people to help you organize and keep the new data about yourself that initial, accurate reflections bring. I call this individual or group your "witness." A witness will help you build internal storage space so that you can keep successes and new images of yourself readily visible and easily retrievable.

A witness might be a therapist (see discussion in the next section); an accepting friend, or a mentor; a support group, coach, or even a professional organizer.

Start with one new person who understands AD/HD or with whom you can identify. It might be a new role model or just someone who has the ability to accept and see the real you. You must find somebody to identify with, whether at an AD/HD conference, in an on-line AD/HD chat room, or in another safe environment.

Your witness might be a person who doesn't have AD/HD but who is different from the mainstream in many of the same important ways that you are. This individual might be adventurous or freethinking or creative or passionate about a certain subject or reflective or sensitive; whatever the trait (or traits), you can see it in yourself as well. When you spend time with this person, you feel relaxed, accepted, and respected.

I have seen firsthand how support groups can function as excellent witnesses. The advantage of groups is that they put you on freeze-frame so you can focus on your small successes and begin to build on them. As a result, a fuller picture of yourself will gradually emerge, like a Polaroid picture slowly coming into view. When you have developed the capacity to store positive reflections and build on them, when you have begun to value your differences, you are approaching the marker of true acceptance.

When Sandra first joined an AD/HD support group, she was shy and self-deprecating. Even though obviously talented, she had lost confidence and sight of her true abilities. With the ongoing support of the group, she took one small step toward establishing her career. Over a period of time,

Sandra had one success after another in her field, but because of a distorted self-image she continued to downplay or overlook her successes. The group members, however, were able to recognize her success and made her pause and look at it. These witnesses tracked her steps until she saw it and acknowledged to herself that she had become a well-respected member of her profession.

A distorted self-image dies hard and often lags behind our experiences and growth. Changing your self-view to match reality takes a long time. Sometimes, as in Sandra's case, your external progress can be so rapid that you and others who have known you for years have trouble keeping up with it; but even if your progress comes at a more moderate speed, you should be aware that your old self-image may be hard to shake—for you and for others. It may stubbornly hang around until a witness finally makes you sit down and face your real accomplishments.

Positive Reflections in Therapy

Choosing helpful counseling at particular junctures along the journey can be an effective way for individuals to build the positive feedback loops we have been discussing. A good therapist will help you move toward a new view of your self and your own possibilities—not merely help you adjust to your limitations.

If you hesitate to seek out positive reflections in a larger context—such as support groups, seminars, retreats—you might consider doing some one-on-one work with a therapist who understands AD/HD in all its forms, with whom you feel safe and in partnership or any counselor who listens and respects your differences, even if she or he has no expertise in adult AD/HD.

As a client, you should feel respected, not marginalized. Your AD/HD does not make you less intelligent or more disturbed than the population at large.

When Beth first came to see me, she was focusing exclusively on her deficits. Not only could she not see her strengths, but she clearly believed that her deficits made her a bad or flawed person. "I'm a slob at work," she said. "I'm so stupid with organizing my files." Beth needed to see that she was characterizing herself exclusively in the negative, wiping away any view of her strengths. To show her this, I encouraged her to describe her difficulties in more neutral language. For example, instead of the above, she said, "I have problems with keeping things arranged on my desktop" and "I have difficulties with organizing my files." Saying these statements laid the groundwork for communicating this information to others at a later time.

Therapists and friends of adults like Beth, who are especially sensitive about their difficulties, should also encourage them to talk about their strengths along with their deficits. Over time, Beth learned to think to herself and eventually to say, "I'm really good at doing the layout and design of the office newsletter, even if I have a hard time writing it." Now Beth was talking about her strengths and difficulties in the same breath and would soon be able to see that they were all part of who she was. Her difficulties did not take away her enjoyment of and facility with the more creative tasks at work. The one did not cancel out the other.

•

As we saw in the previous chapter, Lance had struggled all his life to deny his deficits because the prospect of letting others see them made him feel too vulnerable. Consequently, he did not see the areas where he needed support and often let people down. As a result, he had come to believe that he was irresponsible. Lance needed someone to help him see and accept his deficits and to show him that these deficits did not cancel out his value as a person. Only then would he be able to communicate his needs to others and begin to seek out help. The process of beginning to let in support touched the core of his identity and therefore proceeded at a slow pace.

Like other adults with AD/HD, Lance had not gone to therapy to work on his self-concept. He was trying to cope with the fact that his life was a mess on both professional and personal levels. But before I could show him how his difficulty in facing his areas of weakness was contributing to the severity of his situation, I needed to gain his trust. I had to communicate my acceptance of him while reflecting back to him some of his difficulties. I had to make him understand that I could see both his talents and difficulties at the same time, and that they didn't define who he was.

For example, I said to him: "You clearly have talents and produce some of the finest work in your field. At the same time, your persistent problems with staff and billing don't seem to be going away, and you have not been able to deliver products to your customers on time. This must be tremendously frustrating." Gradually, over a period of months, in which I reflected both his strengths and his deficits, Lance was able to see his whole self and that his deficits did not invalidate his strengths.

The goal was for him to be able to say, "I have talents *but* I need support." (That's a little different from what Don and Beth needed to learn to say: "I am a creative person *even though* I have trouble with things.") He had to learn to say to himself, "I am very creative. I have difficulty with projects getting done on time. I have difficulty keeping records and meeting deadlines." Such statements amount to accurate descriptions, rather than positive or negative characterizations.

Lance's challenge was to let someone besides me see a few of his deficits in the course of a conversation. He might say, for example, "Boy, I find it's really difficult to meet these deadlines. I have a lot of trouble doing timelines." Then he could balance this with something positive, like "I get so absorbed in the quality of my work or so involved in helping the client or creating a great event that it's hard for me to pull back." Or "I love my work, I'm proud of it, but the administrative aspects of it are really an area of tremendous challenge for me. Do you have any ideas about how I could get some better help?"

After a while, Lance was able to speak more openly with his sister, a person he had always trusted, about his difficulties. When he saw that she was not judgmental, but supportive and eager to help, Lance gained courage and gradually began to communicate his particular challenges to his secretary. This was a huge step, since he was now able to clearly ask for help where he needed it most and, for the first time in years, accept his secretary's help when she offered it.

At the same time, Lance's need for high stimulation meant that he continued to take on too much and had difficulty setting boundaries with people. So he still found himself living occasionally on the edge of a crash. Except now he was able to ask for help when he took the time and space to communicate. He still needed to work on achieving more balance in life, a subject we will explore in Journey Three.

True Acceptance

Once you have developed explanatory and valuing voices, gathered new experiences of yourself, collected accurate reflections, and expanded your self-view to include the whole picture of yourself—strengths and deficits together—you will most likely be at a place of deeper acceptance of yourself and your differences.

In the last twelve years of working with adults, I have noticed that those who finally reach true acceptance have separated their core definition of themselves from their AD/HD. This pivotal point isn't the moment their desks become orderly. It comes as part of the gradual process of internalizing new experiences and learning to see themselves outside the limiting context of their AD/HD. While these adults still struggle with their deficits—which continue to frustrate, confuse, or restrict them in some way—they arrive at a point where they can see their strengths and talents, along with their weaknesses. This expanded view leaves them free to begin succeeding in their lives in a way they have not been able to do when they lived with self-distortion. Once you reach true acceptance, you will be more willing to take action despite your AD/HD difficulties.

Another sign of true acceptance is that you're willing to let your AD/HD be visible and share this part of yourself rather than hide it.

On one occasion when my AD/HD struck, I noticed right before my clients began to show up for a group counseling session that I had on mismatched shoes. I had been wearing them all day. (At least they were both black!) It was too late to go home to change. I could have made up an excuse, feigned sudden illness, as I might have done at an earlier stage of the journey. But instead I sat down in my usual place in the circle, and pointed to my shoes, and said, "OOPS."

To my surprise, not only did the whole group have a good laugh over my small blunder, but the situation turned out to be very therapeutic for my clients. Until then, all our talk of deficits and strengths and revising our self-view had been nothing more than theory. But here they saw that I too struggled with the same difficulties they experienced. They also saw that I had reached a point where I no longer let this be a roadblock to the rest of my life. Later, this incident became an inside joke with many of my clients. They also confided to me that in this session they had experienced one of the most important breakthroughs of their treatment.

True acceptance marks the midpoint of Journey Two. When you have reached true acceptance, you will no longer feel resigned to your AD/HD or to a life dedicated to battling or hiding your AD/HD symptoms. You will not only see yourself as a whole person apart from your AD/HD, but also realize that your AD/HD is merely a part of you and a challenge. While the difficulties of your AD/HD will not disappear, your ability to live with and adapt to them will increase. Once you have reached true acceptance, you will deal with your difficulties more effectively, use the support of others to organize yourself, and see possibilities for yourself that you might not have imagined at an earlier stage of your travels. A developed self-concept and true acceptance will prepare you to deal with the identity crisis that is often precipitated by true acceptance, to be explored in the following two chapters.

Explorations

Brainstorming is an effective problem-solving strategy that you might find helpful as you move toward true acceptance. Try the following exercise.

- **Write down the names of those people who can see only your deficits. Then write down the names of those who see the whole picture and accept you.**

- **Estimate how much time you spend with each of these two groups.**

- **If a disproportionate amount of time is spent with those who see only your deficits, ask yourself where you can find more people who will be accepting of you.**

- **Are there other groups where people might tend to be more like you?**

- **Consider AD/HD gatherings—local, regional, national, on-line.**

Adults in pseudo-acceptance often define their goal in terms of eliminating their symptoms and getting over the AD/HD. For those in true acceptance, this goal is no longer a defining marker.

To determine whether you are genuinely at the point of true acceptance, see if the following statements apply to you.

- **I no longer feel the need to be fixed.**

- **I see that one of the central goals of my journeys with AD/HD is not to fix myself but to expand my self-view and my life.**

- **My aim is not to change, alter, or delete parts of myself. It is literally to develop and strengthen what is already there.**

5

Facing an Identity Crisis

WHILE OTHER YOUNG ADULTS were starting out and reshaping, refining, molding, remolding, adjusting their choices, self-images and dreams, you may have reached adulthood with a gap in information about yourself that didn't allow you to do that initial bit of reality testing and adjustment.

As a result of your AD/HD, you may have held on tightly to dreams that were slowly being submerged little by little, year after year, until they were just treasures lost at the bottom of your soul. Most likely, you felt that there was no way to retrieve your dreams and restore their former sparkle. You may have kept pining for these dreams nonetheless, or perhaps you put all thoughts of them out of your mind.

By this point in Journey Two, you may experience some confusion that amounts to an identity crisis. The identity crisis begins roughly in the middle of this journey after you achieve true acceptance of your real self but begin to question the authenticity of your life. You may feel that your life no longer fits your newly developed and expanded self-view. You may feel uncertain about the future and what you want to do with your new understanding of yourself. To resolve this identity crisis, you will need to revisit a difficult and painful time in your past. You almost have to go back to where you fell off the developmental road and complete that process now that you have more complete information that you lacked then. This process will ultimately give you the means to construct a vision for the rest of your life.

As we saw in the last two chapters, adults with AD/HD often build their lives around flawed data and ideas about themselves. Beth had gone into secretarial work because she believed developing and mastering organizational skills should be the central marker of success in life. Don went into the insurance business without ever questioning whether this line of work would reward and satisfy his creative side. Lance went into business for himself before he was able to clearly see his deficits and understand how his drive to take on too much, coupled with his attention problems, would make owning and running his own business difficult for him. As for Jennifer, the housewife and mother, she had lived a life of struggling to clean and organize her household without ever questioning whether this life was a good fit for her.

But as adults see more of themselves, the lives that they have constructed may not quite fit their new self-concepts. As Don spent more and more evenings with the friends he had made from his poetry discussion group, he began to wonder why he had ever wanted to work in such a conservative, straitlaced industry. Did he really fit in at his company? Was he really suited to be an insurance salesman?

Likewise, after Lance began to see how difficult it was for

him to work alone due to his inability to manage not only himself but others, he began to wonder if he might consider working with someone else, developing a team, or even going to work for a large company, as he had done in his youth. Similarly, as Jennifer continued to escape her house once or twice a week and discovered the pleasure of spending time by herself, she too wondered if she might not want or need to change the shape of her life in some way. Beth also experienced this subtle shift in her life as she rediscovered old friends and began to consider the possibility that completely overcoming her organizational difficulties didn't have to remain the central priority and exclusive focus of her life.

But in what way should these individuals change their lives? Jennifer loved her family and didn't want to change her life in any way that would hurt them. Beth had been a secretary for a long time and was worried about making any quick changes. Don felt that he had no clear course to take. His job paid the bills quite well—he certainly couldn't make a living discussing poetry. And Lance no longer knew what he wanted. He had invested practically his entire adult life in his one-man firm, yet at the same time, he had begun to want more from life than just getting by and barely staying in business.

So what were Jennifer, Beth, Don, and Lance to do? What did their new understandings and view of themselves mean for their lives at this point in their journeys?

The Roadblock of Fear

Remember that these individuals didn't come to treatment complaining of lost dreams. They came wanting to conform, to get rid of these nagging feelings that were coming from somewhere deep within. When I bring up this pain of lost dreams in counseling, and confront people with the possibility of opening up to these feelings, at first they usually deny that their longings even exist. They deny the importance of these feelings, or insist they must get rid of the AD/HD before indulging in such luxuries.

Their reluctance is understandable, because they've already had so much disappointment. Dreams are fragile, and you want to protect them and keep them undisturbed, like a crying infant who finally falls into a peaceful sleep. There may be the fear that your dreams will be destroyed once again, that success will explode in your face as it has in the past.

You may fear you won't be able to keep up any success you do manage to achieve and that you will ultimately disappoint yourself and others one more time. Or perhaps the pressure would be too intense. Since you feel you couldn't bear that again, you may have settled for just continuing what is by now your familiar focus on controlling your "negative" AD/HD symptoms.

Many people with AD/HD know they have much to give or contribute, but can see no way to fulfill their potential. One man described to me his pain and frustration, saying it was as if he spent all day every day building beautiful and intricate sand castles on the shore, only to have them washed away each day. Another bright and creative individual told me that living with AD/HD was like being given a "life sentence of inefficiency."

Even success leads to pressure for them, because they don't think they can continue to perform up to expectations. They run up against their own fears and insecurities. Often, when

> *And then the day came when the risk to remain tight in a bud was more painful than the risk it took to blossom.*
>
> —Anaïs Nin

an adult with AD/HD considers acting on a strength or talent, she will have a knee-jerk response of fear and retreat from good opportunities because she has vivid and unpleasant memories of earlier failures in similar situations.

Reawakening the Pain of Unfulfilled Dreams

At the same time that these individuals begin to look forward to uncertain futures, something surprising and not always comfortable happens. They begin to remember a particularly painful time of their lives when, as prediagnosed young people, their dreams crumbled and their lives—sometimes suddenly, sometimes gradually and without explanation—seemed to have collapsed.

As Don enjoyed his new friends more and more, he began to remember a time in his life when he believed he might become a poet. Now that he was experiencing his strengths again, he could not help but remember this earlier time when he had once tried to act on the same strengths. Lance, Beth, and Jennifer also began to remember similar points in their past, when they had tried to act on their strengths but somehow gone far off track.

Even though remembering such a time can be painful and scary, when you know to expect it, this revisiting of the past is a healthy and inevitable part of Journey Two. Your task at this point is to face the pain of old dreams or of parts of yourself left behind. Only by looking back and facing this pain will you gradually begin to see your future and resolve your identity crisis.

Finding the Source of Pain

To understand how this pain will move you through your identity crisis, you will first need to understand where it comes from and why it is at times so frightening to face.

Although undiagnosed children who have AD/HD usually experience difficulties, some also glimpse and experience their strengths and gifts. Not only is this true for those, like Lance, who tend to overemphasize their strengths, but it is also true for individuals who distort their weaknesses. Beth was praised for her design abilities and won a summer internship at an advertising agency. As a young adult, Don had begun publishing his poems in national literary magazines. Jennifer, the housewife who identified solely with how well she kept house, used to be an outgoing teen who had many close friendships and volunteered her time to several charities.

Just like other young adults, these individuals had been exploring the range of their gifts and had begun to excel and blossom. Unlike their peers, however, at some point, little by little, perhaps imperceptibly at first, their dreams slipped away. Without further consideration of past strengths, without careful thought or understanding of the whole picture, Don eventually became an insurance salesman; Lance started his own company, which he could barely keep afloat; Jennifer became an exhausted housewife without a social life; and Beth repeatedly failed as a secretary. Unfortunately, their stories are not at all uncommon among adults who grow up undiagnosed. But what became of the dreams and aspirations of these adults? How did Don transform from talented poet to an insurance salesman, and how did Jennifer go from a social young woman to a tired and self-critical wife and mother without an identity of her own, apart from her view of herself as a failure in these roles?

As discussed earlier, children with undiagnosed AD/HD are often able to succeed early on because of strong support systems made up of teachers, parents, and friends. Lance had a doting mother who kept her son's room clean and made sure that his books and assignments were in order so that he could pursue his many different areas of interest without any distractions. Like Lance, Don was fortunate to have the same support from his parents, as well as a caring English teacher who saw his talent early on, encouraged him, and even took time after class to help him with mechanical problems—spelling and punctuation—which might have otherwise crippled Don early on. When they were girls, homework and chores around the house took Jennifer and Beth considerably more time than was usual, but their support systems enabled them to have enough time and energy to pursue other activities and interests. With the help of such support systems as well as the reduced responsibility and obligations of early life, many young people undiagnosed with AD/HD, especially those who are exceptionally bright or creative or personable, find their strengths and act on them.

Later, when these individuals leave home and begin taking on more responsibilities without a support system in place, their dreams slowly crumble as they hit what feels like a wall. Still worse, they have no explanation for their inability to succeed or to take on the same challenges as their peers'. As they drop out of college, fail to pay bills on time, or lose jobs and friends, they stand by and watch as everyone else seems to succeed with much less effort.

Don and Beth hit this wall when they left home to attend college, where they continued to have the same difficulties they experienced in high school. Now, however, they were expected to take on additional responsibilities. Don had to work part-time jobs to help pay for his education. Though Beth's parents were paying all her expenses, she began to flounder as she struggled with the added responsibilities of writing monthly checks, shopping for groceries, doing her laundry, and just maintaining a life outside of academics. As they struggled with classes and with life in general, they had less and less time and energy to pursue their dreams. Eventually, Don had to drop out of college. As we've seen, Beth had a very difficult time in college, finally completing a two-year program at a community college.

Jennifer, who did finish college, married and had a family, which took all of her time and energy and left her without any life outside of what she saw as her messy home.

On the other hand, Lance continued to excel in college as he had in high school. Now and then, he had near calamities. His room was always a "disaster area," and he often missed classes or was late due to his problems with organization and overloading his schedule. But the exceptionally high quality of his work, along with his outgoing and

> *What Happens to a Dream Deferred?*
>
> —from the poem "A Dream Deferred"
> by Langston Hughes

charming personality, usually made up for his lapses. He hit the wall when, as a recent graduate with great recommendations from professors with whom he had worked on the school paper and on the campus radio show, he took a job at a top public relations firm. This job had been his lifelong dream; he had spent years imagining the excitement of the work, the status it would bring him, the challenge of working his way up the corporate ladder.

He excelled, and his work was praised. However, he repeatedly missed deadlines and was unable to comply with his firm's record-keeping rules. After many warnings, he was fired. For the first time that he could remember, no exceptions were made because of his talent. He emptied out his desk and vowed that he would never work with or for anyone else again. From now on, he would be his own boss and rely on no one.

Perhaps what makes the unrealized dreams of adults with AD/HD especially painful is the fact that they once felt so close to achieving them and then, without warning or explanation, moved off track completely. Even as Don, for example, struggled in college, he continued to get strong support from English professors who had read his essays and found his work brilliant. But when he repeatedly failed to hand in assignments on time, they could not give him a passing grade. Even though he dropped out of college, he continued to write poetry on his own. After a few months,

Don began to have problems making money. It was at this point that his dream seemed to come true. A local community art center in need of a poetry teacher hired him.

Don's vision for his life then was to support himself teaching while he wrote his poetry. He had, it seemed to him for a time, achieved his goals. He was writing poetry and paying his bills by teaching the art he practiced. Unfortunately, Don, who had not been diagnosed yet, was about to fail due to a condition he did not even know he had. As a teacher, he was passionate, and his students liked him. But despite his efforts, he often arrived late and spent a great deal of class time trying to get his notes in order. When he reapplied to teach the next semester, the school administrators told him they could not hire him again due to these problems. Don's dreams seemed to have collapsed before his eyes.

Hitting this wall leaves many prediagnosed adults feeling hopeless. Without any way to understand their failure, they come to believe that they simply do not have the talent, intelligence, or whatever else it takes to succeed. They bury their dreams and come to think about them as something they would have achieved had they only been good enough. As they pursue other paths, often less suited to their interests and strengths, the prospect of realizing these dreams becomes ever more distant. Sometimes these old dreams become precious secrets, fantasies that are treasured but never seen as realizable goals or as being relevant to their lives. In other cases, adults forget about their early failures as a way of avoiding the pain associated with that time, even though they could hold important clues for leading more satisfying lives.

After his failure as a teacher and without a viable way of

making money, Don gave up poetry completely and looked for jobs doing anything, so long as it did not remind him of poetry and his failure to succeed. Finally, an insurance company, desperate for help, hired him as a salesperson. As he put all his energy into filling out his sales reports, his old dream faded. In fact, he no longer even read poetry, much less attended readings or discussed the subject with friends, as the topic conjured up painful memories. Sometimes, in the evenings after work, Don fantasized about what might have happened if he had succeeded. He even saw himself giving readings, signing books. But these were just fantasies, he told himself, and he never mentioned them to his colleagues or, even in the first months of therapy, to me. He guarded these thoughts carefully.

Later, when he was diagnosed, he was told, as many adults are, to "focus on his strengths." But by this time, Don's old dream was a distant fantasy; he felt it represented weakness instead of strength. The young man who had once pursued poetry, Don felt, had been foolish. It was no longer who he was. Though he was not particularly fulfilled or happy, Don felt that his life was good enough.

Letting the Pain of Old Dreams Guide You

After years of living inauthentic lives, many adults with AD/HD no longer have a strong sense of what matters to them, what might give their lives direction, meaning, and joy. Before they are diagnosed, they're always so overwhelmed and spend so much time coping with their AD/HD. But even after receiving treatment for their primary symptoms, they're unable to automatically pick up the pieces. This is partly because they have buried their dreams and the vitality that accompanies them. In fact, many adults forget how important these dreams once were to them. They may even forget that they ever had dreams in the first place.

After she had pursued secretarial work for three years, Beth barely remembered the joy and satisfaction she had once gotten from art. Similarly, after Lance had been fired from his large public relations firm and begun his frazzled plunge into self-employment, he no longer recalled the satisfaction that the status of his earlier job and the collegiality of the other employees had once given him. When his chaotic life of self-employment led to his divorce and separation from his kids, he told himself he had only been meant to work, that family and love were not for him. In fact, Lance had always wanted a family and longed to be a good father. But after these failures, he gave up these dreams and lost still more vitality.

The challenge for the adult at this point in Journey Two is to recover some of this vitality and joy by reconsidering old, submerged dreams. This is not to say that you should try again to achieve the exact goals in the same form that you once envisioned, but that old dreams may suggest very real directions for your future. For now, you need to explore what you once wanted for yourself in order to see if these old yearnings still matter to you.

But if your dreams have been buried, lost, forgotten, how are you to reconnect with them? The key to recovering them is in the pain that you may still associate with your early failure. This is why I tell my clients who have achieved acceptance and have entered the identity crisis to pay attention to the pain of these old dreams. In short, you now need to let the pain of old dreams guide you. It will lead you back to what once mattered to you and, despite all your attempts to convince yourself otherwise, what still matters to you on some level.

You may find yourself withdrawing whenever you feel the pain of old dreams. You may find yourself seeing in your old dreams a Pandora's box. You fear that if you open this box and look inside, you'll let all the old difficulties and struggles back into your life. This fear is perfectly understandable. But once you have expanded your self-concept, you are ready to face this pain and even to begin thinking about succeeding again. You are much more capable of making constructive decisions and positioning yourself for success.

All you have to do to start this process is to notice those yearnings, pangs, and stings when they occur. This pain may occasionally flit across your mind. You may feel it in your heart or stomach for an instant before it leaves again. You may not even know where it comes from at first. It may seem to come out of nowhere and land on top of you or hang over you like a cloud. Such feelings may come at unexpected times—perhaps right in the middle of an ordinary day. If you have reached this point in your travels, you will understand that these pangs are important messages like hunger pains that signal you to eat in order to protect you from starvation, or sleepiness that ensures you will rest. These pangs are different from ordinary sadness or anxiety. They signal you to pay attention because they may point you to yourself, to old dreams, to wishes and desires and goals you may want to put to rest or to resuscitate.

BETH REMEMBERS HER DREAM OF BEING A GRAPHIC DESIGNER

Beth started to feel the pain of old dreams not long after she began to spend more and more free time with her friends. She had already come to realize that secretarial work was not a good fit and hence not a good path for her to pursue, though she also had no idea what else she could do. At the same time, Beth noticed that she was somewhat defensive around Mary, an old friend from college. At first Beth did not understand her defensiveness, since she was very fond of Mary. I asked Beth to examine the feelings she associated with Mary. Whenever she felt this defensiveness, it would be helpful for Beth to ask herself what she might be responding to.

Before long, Beth noticed that every time Mary brought up her success as a photographer—a gallery recently had shown her work—Beth would become quiet and with-drawn or might try to change the subject. Beth soon under-stood that she was remembering her own letting go of her original aspirations and early successes in graphic design and even feeling a little envious toward Mary. She began to notice that she responded similarly toward anything that re-minded her of her earlier attempts at art and design. For ex-ample, she felt little pangs when she looked at magazines and saw a good layout for an advertisement, and she would often even feel a little down as she passed certain billboards on her way to work. Now Beth began to feel a number of emotions—pain, regret, loss—that were difficult for her to face. But as she did so, she came to realize that art, design es-pecially, meant a great deal to her. She now had something to work with, something that might help her begin to shape and envision her future.

ACKNOWLEDGING MY YEARNINGS FOR RECOGNITION

Before diagnosis, but after I was a therapist, every time I at-tended a large professional conference, every time I saw a person wearing a blue speaker's ribbon, I felt feelings of loss. I coveted those speakers' ribbons, for whoever wore them seemed to be saying to the world, "I have something important to say." When the conference was over and I went back to work, I would feel sad and demoralized.

My therapist at the time encouraged me to use these feelings as signs of what was important for me to work toward. Rather than leading to a downward spiral of discouragement, these pangs could point me in the direction of my true desires and capabilities—serve as valuable motivation to get me moving in that direction. I began to welcome these signals and listen to them. (Ultimately, I was able to act on them and to earn my own blue ribbon.)

If You're Feeling Stuck...

If you find yourself stuck at this point and unable to go forward, you need to go back and determine whether what may have passed for acceptance is actually resignation. Like Don, Beth, and many other adults with AD/HD who have hit the wall and experienced what they see as significant failure or disappointment in their lives, you may believe that you have achieved acceptance when, in fact, you are still seeing yourself too much in terms of your deficits.

It may be resignation if you feel the diagnosis means you must settle for a lesser reality. Don was resigned to the fact—or so he thought—that he simply was not gifted enough to ever become a poet. If you feel you must or should discard wishes for the life you wanted, or discard who you thought you were, you are resigned. In this case, what you are *actually* accepting is that you are deficient. You may often feel that to be successfully treated for AD/HD means you must "accept" your fate. However, it is not until you have achieved true acceptance that you are able to

There *is* something worse than the pain of AD/HD; it is the pain of the death of dreams, of meaning and self. To give up the part of yourself that expresses what you most care about or need to express is to die inside. Many people learn to keep their eyes down permanently so as not to burn up by flying too close to the sun. This may make you feel safe, but, on the other hand, you will never see the sun again. You will live a life without light.

move on and resolve the identity issues that continually and increasingly pop up after diagnosis.

You may be unable to move on because you're afraid to face the pain you're unleashing. You may want to withdraw, as you did in the past. You have fears of the unknown road ahead as you progress toward new experiences and encounter unforeseen obstacles. The danger here is that you will become too afraid and turn back to an old familiar, even if unsatisfying, pathway.

If such fears are holding you back, you may need the support of a trusted guide, such as a therapist or coach. As coach Hope Langner puts it, "As a coach, I see myself holding a flashlight for my clients, shining it where they need to look to discover what's next, and then supporting them to take the steps they need to take to move forward."

I remember the time when Don's fears threatened to sabotage his progress. Not too long after he started attending meetings of the poetry discussion group, his old dream was brought back to him when a new friend from this group asked him, out of the blue, if he had ever written poetry. Don felt immediately defensive and protective and merely said that he had once tried it. After this conversation, Don actually stopped attending the discussion group.

When he brought this up in therapy, I was able to assure him that his pain was a natural and inevitable part of the voyage and that if he followed it he might discover this old part of himself that could be a key to his future. Though he was still anxious for a while, Don gradually began to open up to his poetry again. For the first time, he told me about his early attempts with writing, his publications, and the fact that he had given it up. That these memories were scary and painful for him. After confronting his fears, Don was able to go back to his group and even began to consider seeking out a writing group in order to reconnect with his interest in writing. Even though he did not yet act on this thought, he had made a huge leap forward. With the help of a guide, he began to see how the pain of old failures could awaken new possibilities.

Not All Dreams Are About Achievement

While for many adults this part of Journey Two is about re-membering some specific goal or set of goals that they failed to realize, for others it is not about achievement at all. If it is this way for you, you may feel a bit confused as you wonder what it is that you failed to do and that you might do once you have achieved acceptance. Rest assured that you are not lost if you feel this way. Remember that your ultimate goal is not achievement but rather to live authentically. For many adults, such as Jennifer, the goal at this point is to remember a time in their lives when they felt more vital, more alive, when they seemed to laugh more, dance about the room, experience pleasure in going to concerts, museums, or just out to coffee with friends. These adults need to try and un-derstand how to tap into this lost vitality again.

In the next chapter, you will use the meaning of your old dreams—whatever they may be—to construct a new vision that is relevant to your present life. In this way, you will identify your crisis.

Staying away from pain will hold you back at some point. Dealing with it too early will overwhelm you. But at the right point in your journey, you must confront these feelings and find a way to satisfy your longings. Let them inspire and drive you. The more you listen to them, the more you'll hear the quiet sounds and muffled voice become louder, letting you know that *you're in there somewhere* and trying to get out.

Explorations

Remember, at this point you need to begin reading your own signals instead of pushing them away. Welcome the hurt, the feelings of loss; let them serve as your guide. You will be following the clues—your memories and associations—that you have left behind like bread crumbs to lead you back home to yourself.

When these feelings appear, put them on pause, enhance them, make them bigger. Capture the feeling, the memory, for at least a moment, so it registers and makes an impression.

Don't be concerned if you can't completely understand these feelings at first. The picture will develop and become clearer later in your voyage. Meanwhile, here are some tips for understanding the core meaning of past pain.

- **Keep a diary. Write down what was happening at the time when you felt one of these pangs or feelings of longing. Write down what you remembered, what picture you saw, what you felt.**

- **What scares you about examining your past dreams?**

- Pay attention to what happens as your feelings break through to the surface. Are you pushing them down as soon as they appear?

- Hold on to these feelings a second longer than usual and ask yourself what message they relay. If you don't know what hurts, you won't be able to address it.

- What is stopping you from moving toward those dreams?

6

Resolving the Identity Crisis

OW THAT YOU HAVE OPENED UP to the pain of unrealized dreams, you are ready to construct a new vision of your future. You arrive at your new vision by exploring how you might bring part or all of these dreams into your life. Chances are that both you and your life have changed since the days when you first conceived these dreams. This means that you will now need to find a way to bring your dreams into sync with your present life or *reshape your old dreams*.

As you move through Journey Two and construct a new vision for your life, keep in mind that shifting and reshaping old dreams to fit your present life and your AD/HD is not about giving up grand expectations for lesser ones. It's about making good decisions that will allow you to live the fullest, most personally satisfying life you can. The ability to shift when necessary is not a sign of failure but a sign of success, increasing the likelihood of the realization of your dreams.

As you work through this process, you will resolve your identity crisis and may return to a vitality that you may not have felt for years. You'll then begin to experiment with

v vision in the world, taking small steps toward ac-
ᴀ finding, entering, and living in what I call your
ᴜnique zone.

The extent to which you will have to reshape your vision will depend on you. Some adults may find that their
old dreams are not outdated and, with minimal adjustments, still fit who they've become. This may be true for individuals who were relatively young at the time of diagnosis
and who feel that they still have the time and energy to
make their lives work with their original dreams. While this
is not always possible for adults who are diagnosed with
AD/HD later, there are always ways to work toward a more
fulfilling life.

Back to the Future

I break this process of shifting and reshaping down into
three steps:

- **Understand the core elements of earlier
  dreams that still hold meaning for you.**

- **Transform the pain of old losses into a
  vision of the future, into a new form that
  fits for today but that takes into account
  and blends the past, present, and future.**

- **Begin to act on this new vision by
  experimenting in various ways. You'll
  start to feel a renewed passion for life.**

The dream is always running ahead.

—Anaïs Nin

This process of identifying the core elements of old dreams and then adapting these dreams for today is complex, and it should not be undertaken until you have expanded your self-concept. Otherwise it will be too frightening for you. You must see yourself as a whole person if you are to clearly see both the person you once were and the person you are now and finally integrate these two pictures in a way that will continue to lead you into a satisfying future. This is a slow, organic process that cannot be hurried, though it can be helped by putting the right building blocks into place. Those who are ready to take on this task will probably know it because the hitherto daunting task of letting go of and changing earlier dreams won't feel as overwhelming or impossible.

Identifying the Core Elements of Your Dreams

To update your dreams, begin by answering the following questions:

- **What kernels of those original dreams still matter to you?**

- **What parts of your original dreams are useful to you today? What parts of them are hopelessly out of date?**

- **What parts simply won't fit with your present life, and what parts will?**

The process of seeing the core of old dreams that you do want to reshape sometimes means that you will need to let go of and mourn the original form of those dreams. For years, our parents told us to "grow up and face reality." No wonder so many of us hold on so tightly to our dreams. We have been taught that they are unrealistic and that the of all the magic they hold for us is this harsh life called "reality." In fact, this is anything but the case. Judith Viorst writes in her book *Necessary Losses*, "A sense of reality lets us access ourselves and the world with relative accuracy. Accepting reality means that we've come to terms with the world's and our own limitations and flaws. It also means establishing achievable goals for ourselves, compromises, and substitutes that we put in place of our earlier longings (p. 185)."

KEEPING MY DREAMS ALIVE

As I look back to the years before my own diagnosis, I remember feeling the pain that we discussed in the previous chapter and not knowing what it was connected to. For months, I experienced seemingly inexplicable feelings at odd times, triggered by a variety of situations.

Sometimes this would happen right in the middle of watching Peter Jennings report on the evening news or while watching a TV magazine show anchored by Diane Sawyer. Then these feelings, or pangs, began to occur while reading about or watching anyone who had achieved some level of visibility or who was expressing herself publicly. The feelings would rise up suddenly like a wave, leaving me awash in gloom. Later, I came to understand these pangs as a sense of loss.

After diagnosis and once I acknowledged this sense of loss, I wondered how I was supposed to understand its significance for my life. Did I really want to become a newsperson or a TV personality? What was it that was keeping me from watching the news? What was the issue I had not worked through? What exactly was still in there, giving me a good swift kick every once in a while?

I had to go back and remember how in college years earlier I enjoyed my classes in communications, specifically radio and TV. I recalled the point at which I let go of that dream and that interest without carefully analyzing or exploring my choices in any meaningful way.

Later on, I began to understand that for me there was something about communications that expressed my deepest desires and abilities. I knew I didn't want to go back to school and become a broadcaster at midlife, but it took some time for me to figure out that what was still alive in me was the desire to make myself heard, to reach out to people and affect them in some way. In other words, my past dream was telling me something about who I was and what my longings were.

Once I had identified the elements at the core of my dream, I could begin to transform my dream and integrate it into my present. I gradually constructed a vision of my future that would include writing and public speaking about a topic that I knew and cared a great deal about. Had I not been far enough along in my journey, the pain of my lost dream probably would not have been useful to me. Had I not been able to see myself clearly and fully, I might never have been able to see the core of this dream. I would simply have focused on the loss.

Jennifer Remembers Her Lighter Side

Unlike Beth, Don, and Lance, Jennifer never had any professional aspirations. A mother in her late thirties, she loved her two children and her husband and had never felt that she wanted to work or have a career. After expanding and correcting her distorted view of herself, Jennifer did not quite know how to approach the issues of revisiting old dreams. Since she had never really wanted to accomplish anything specific, she felt for a while as if she had no sense of passion and vitality to revive. It seemed as if she could barely remember what she wanted as a young woman. Given that Jennifer, as a housewife and mother, was living the life she had always envisioned for herself, what was it she needed to bring into the future? What was it that went off track for her? What dreams had been deeply buried? What parts of herself had become submerged and now needed to be reengaged? If Jennifer was to continue on her journey with new vitality, she would need to answer these crucial questions.

To help Jennifer along, I asked her if she had felt any regret or remembered a time in her life that was particularly precious to her now. For a number of weeks, Jennifer drew a blank on this question. But as she thought about it, she realized that now and then she experienced a sense of longing and regret when she saw other women enjoying themselves, relaxing, talking, reading a book, in the café that she visited alone once a week. She began to remember a time when, as a young single woman, she had seemed to enjoy life in a more carefree way than she did now. As we worked together, Jennifer saw that this freer part of herself, the part that had been able to relax, enjoy free time, sit in the sun or under a tree and think, had been buried beneath layers of guilt. This was the side of her that, at one time, she believed had distracted her from her domestic duties, the side that she could not have if she was also to be a model mother and wife. Jennifer had believed for so many years that opening herself up to this lost experience of herself would be pointless and just cause pain. But once she had allowed herself to feel the pain of this loss, she was able to identify her dream.

Now she could start thinking about how to integrate it into a new vision for her future.

USING FANTASIES TO GET TO THE CORE OF YOUR DREAMS

Some fantasies are truly wonderful to keep and enjoy. We keep them secret, hide them away, cherish them, and nurture them. We take them out on rainy days when we need to dream and escape. They don't need to make sense or be brought into line with today's reality. We just need to know the difference between these fantasies and real-life dreams.

To illustrate how fantasies can be useful, I like to use the example of how some adults tend to idealize an early love. Imagine you've been nurturing an image of an old boyfriend or girlfriend you haven't seen for twenty years. These kinds of fantasies are fun and harmless unless they hold you back from your real life. But what if for years no one seemed to measure up to this person and so, keeping this ideal in mind, you never settled down with anyone you dated? You see him or her again at the high school reunion and finally have to face the fact that the sixteen-year-old you've been imagining all these years is actually now a middle-aged man or woman.

As a result, you let go of this fantasy and, for the better, begin to "face reality." Wistfully, you realize that the dream of running off with your first love to a desert island you used to imagine when your life seemed a little boring isn't going to work anymore. You realize that this dream is over and that you don't really want this person in your life anymore. While this realization may seem sad, it is also freeing, because now you can begin to look for a partner who would be right for you in real life.

You held on to the ideal image of your first love because there was something about this person that you really treasured and needed. Now that you have stopped fantasizing, you need to ask yourself why you thought so much about this individual over the years. Was it the excitement, the adventure you two had together? Perhaps it was his or her sense of humor, sensitivity, love of books and music, or particular way of looking at the world. Or maybe it was the security and balance this person brought to your life. Once you begin to answer these questions, you will be able to see the core elements of this ideal person, and, with these in mind, you will be able to go out and find the right person for you, or identify the qualities you want to develop in yourself.

Transforming the Pain

Transforming pain is a process all people with dashed hopes must take on if they do not want to end up bitter or lost in despair. People who move on to lead satisfying lives after the loss of a dream that represented an important part of their identity eventually find a different route or a new identity. Whether it's a career one has dreamed of that hasn't materialized, or the pain of an infertile couple, acceptance is not about getting over it or becoming resigned to a less happy fate. It's about living with both realities. It's often about mourning and remembering and missing—but then transforming the loss, finding a way to redirect the same impulses or energies.

For example, after coming to grips with the loss of not being able to conceive their own child, a couple may decide to help other infertile couples. They may opt to adopt a child or channel their creative energies into an entirely different realm. These new ways of living don't make up for the original loss, the pain of which will never be completely erased, but can bring other, though different, satisfactions in life.

In the same way that I have encouraged you not to wait until you "get over" your AD/HD before you start your life, I also want to encourage you not to wait until you get over the pain completely before you get on with your life and begin constructing a vision for your future. Your pain will probably never go away completely, though it will subside with time and be balanced by the success you experience as you pursue a new vision for yourself.

Even when you have "accepted" your AD/HD and have begun to see new possibilities for your life, it may still hurt when you see others of equal ability doing two or three times as much work as you do in the same length of time or with less chaos, or making twice as much money as you. Living with AD/HD will most likely continue to be at times frustrating, confounding, and difficult or to leave you sometimes feeling disappointed or angry when you see others able to live and maintain the kind of life you have much more trouble with.

Physician and AD/HD expert Steven Copps gives a well-known speech at AD/HD conferences called "Not Exactly the Midas Touch," which is subtitled "Twice as Hard for Half as Much." This subtitle strikes me as a very accurate description of the pain and frustration of having AD/HD. It is frustrating to work so much longer to produce the same amount, even though the payoff may often be better in the end because of the struggle. I read recently about an experiment in which researchers wanted to see what would happen to butterflies that were taken out of their cocoons by hand. They compared these butterflies with those that had emerged from their cocoons naturally—that is, with a struggle—and the consensus was that those that had struggled were much more beautiful.

So there are benefits that result from the struggle with AD/HD, such as perseverance or empathy for the difficulties of others. Many individuals with AD/HD have found a way to lead satisfying lives. They just keep trying new strategies at the same time that they keep on doing what they need to do to express themselves in their own unique way. In 1998, at the annual conference of the National Attention Deficit Disorder Association (ADDA), I hosted a large gathering of women with AD/HD. On this occasion, many well-known professional women shared their ongoing AD/HD struggles with the audience. It was very empowering and enlightening for all of us to hear that despite such struggles, these women persevere anyway. They don't wait for the time when AD/HD will no longer frustrate them. They have accepted it. Sometimes they hate their AD/HD, sometimes they embrace it, sometimes they enjoy it, but they don't let it stop them. And they accept it because it is just how their brain works, nothing more, nothing less. It doesn't define their value.

Four Different Routes to the Future

When Beth faced the pain of her old dream and began to understand that her early ambition of working in the field of art in some form was still important to her, she looked at her life and began to ask herself whether she might pursue her original dream and go to school in the fine arts. After all, she was single and in her late twenties and had no responsibilities other than herself. So she could conceivably go back to school and pursue this goal.

She revisited her early dream and examined what it was really all about. She discovered some important things. First, she realized that while she had talent in art, what she really loved was the thrill of the business world and commercial art, making things happen as a result of her work. She thought back to the advertising firm where she was an intern during high school. Maybe that was why she kept working as a secretary; she loved being in that atmosphere. She had just picked the wrong outlet. Feeling that she needed security and professional direction in her life, she gave up her fantasy of being an artist on the left bank in Paris. It was a fun fantasy but not one around which she wanted to construct her present life.

As a result of this self-examination process, along with her corrected self-image, Beth was able to identify the core elements of her original dream: She wanted to work with form, and in a creative way that would bring results, in a large exciting firm, and in a way that would also give her financial security. This realization gradually led her in the direction of commercial art. After thinking about many different options, she began to get excited about exploring graphic design and even Web design, which hadn't been an option when she was in college. As she constructed a vision of her future based on an informed knowledge of herself—her strengths, deficits, and longings—she also began to feel an excitement and hopefulness that she had not experienced in years.

Likewise, Don ended up merging his old and new identities and visions with present reality. He was in his late forties

Resolving the Identity Crisis   137

when he finally faced his pain and understood how important poetry was to him. But returning to the old days of living in a single room and struggling to get by was no longer an option for him; he was used to a certain standard of living. At the same time, he knew that his original dream was one that he wanted in some way or form in his life. In his medium-sized town, there were a number of amateur poetry events that he could attend in the evenings. He also thought about moving to the marketing department of his large insurance firm, where he might have the chance to write in-house correspondence and maybe even work on the monthly newsletter that went out to all the employees. Like Beth, he began to experience a new excitement for life once he could envision a better future for himself.

After doing a lot of thinking about his old dream, Lance saw some elements in it that might make his life easier and others that he could keep in his past. Once he understood his deficits, he thought that he should go back to working for a large firm since it would supply the structure he needed. But after working with this idea more, he came to see that his need for high levels of stimulation meant that the structure—set hours, schedules, systems, and procedures—of a large company would soon leave him feeling bored with his work and suffocated by rules. He needed to be free to do what he wanted when he wanted. At the same time, he saw that he currently had too much freedom and that he was often on the brink of bankruptcy because of it. He needed support. He had a hard time managing not only his few employees but also himself. For this reason, he would somehow need to find a compromise between complete self-employment and working for a large company.

He began to imagine scenarios in which he took on a partner who understood him well or in which he worked for a small company that would give him more freedom than a larger company.

When Jennifer reached this stage, she wasn't concerned with performance or success in the traditional sense of these words. Remember: Finding authenticity and meaning—feeling alive again—is not just connected with high performance, outward success, or a thriving career. As we have seen, Jennifer keyed in on the connection and vitality she had experienced as a single person with a lively social life and an active role in her community. It was this part of her life that she wanted back now and that she considered while constructing a new vision for herself. Thoroughly enjoying the two hours she took just for herself each week, she now wanted to take more time to explore a wider range of activities, both social and personal. Of course, she also had responsibilities as a wife and mother, which she would have to take into consideration as she tried to arrive at a good balance between her family life and her life away from her family. Jennifer decided that she could triple her time away from home and still maintain this balance. She made a list of three activities that she thought would move her toward more authenticity. She chose volunteer work, yoga, and photography. The first she had done as a young woman, and she had really enjoyed the experience of contributing to her community in this way. The other two had been activities that she had always secretly wanted to try but had never had the time for. Just by envisioning this plan for herself, Jennifer began to feel energized. She was beginning to shape her life in a way that meant something to her. She, along with Don, Lance, and Beth, was beginning to experience the return to vitality that marks the end of Journey Two.

Resistance to Shifting

A few years ago, I was relaxing in my hotel room before giving a presentation on self-image makeovers at an AD/HD conference. I was flipping through the TV channels when I came across the *Oprah Winfrey Show*. Coincidentally, the subject that afternoon was professional makeovers, and one lucky woman in the audience had just been selected for a complete makeover from head to toe. Oprah was interviewing the woman, who looked as if she hadn't changed her hairstyle or makeup since the 1950s. Even though she was obviously in middle age, she still had her long ponytail. The woman knew intellectually that this change would probably be for the best, but in the end, despite being encouraged and cheered on by the audience, she declined, saying she was just too afraid of the kind of impact such a radical change in her appearance would make in her life. She knew the makeover would not merely be superficial but would affect her entire identity.

Similarly, you may feel great resistance toward shifting to a different life plan since it represents such a fundamental shift in the way you have always seen yourself, even if your old vision is not working well anymore. If, for example, you have always thought you would be a lawyer, and especially if you have invested many years in the pursuit of this goal, working in another field has come to represent "less than" status to you. What is called for at this time is a redefinition of who you thought you were or what you were always told you would or could be.

The process of shifting needs to be viewed not as a move down but as a lateral move. Shifting doesn't mean stepping down, giving up, or lowering your sights. It means you have found a different way to express that core piece of yourself. A successful shift transfers your talents and abilities and the core of your early dreams to another area, one that is not less demanding or challenging or satisfying, even though it is different.

Individuals who see these kinds of shifts as failures have probably not yet achieved acceptance. As a result, they will not be able to continue to move through this stage. These adults remind me of a character in Neil Simon's play *Lost in Yonkers*. Every time the sister in that play enters a new situation, she exclaims disappointedly, "It's not the way I pictured it." Those adults who have the most trouble shifting get hung up on the idea that they never pictured their future this way, staying with that disappointment rather than adjusting or making a new picture now. They want to hold on for dear life to that image they had of who they were supposed to be or what success was in the minds of important people in their life or culture. If they haven't moved into true acceptance yet, they will be afraid that any shift will be the final blow to their self-concept.

Others who work through this obstacle have a freeing experience that allows them to move ahead. They begin to move toward goals born of meaning and authenticity, connecting the past and the future rather than just letting themselves be restricted to or ruled by old dreams. This is the marker that tells you when Journey Two has been successfully navigated.

You don't necessarily have to have AD/HD to feel the need to shift your life's vision in a significant way at some point. James Carville, the intense, hard-driving political strategist often credited for the successful 1992 presidential campaign of Bill Clinton, is an example of someone who made a successful shift in life.

I once heard Carville describe to a group of students how he had been a bad student who went on to be a not-so-great lawyer. Eventually, he realized that were he a client in need of a lawyer, he wouldn't want it to be him. So rather than going through life as a mediocre lawyer, he finally decided to quit the profession.

Carville selected a new field that suited his talents and abilities: his energy, forceful personality, analytical mind, ability to see the whole picture, to strategize brilliantly, and to understand people's motivations. (These qualities are also desirable in an attorney.) He was able to shift successfully in a way that allowed him to capitalize on those strengths and also allowed him to be a fighter and advocate in an even much more forceful way. All these traits added up to quite a different kind of success story and one that has obviously brought him great satisfaction.

Psychiatrist and author John Ratey tells his personal story in the introduction to his book *Shadow Syndromes* (cowritten with Catherine Johnson). He says that his original dream was to be a psychoanalyst. He went through years of study and rigorous training. In many ways he was well suited to the work and enjoyed it until he hit a roadblock. As part of the program requirements, he needed to undergo analysis himself. He found he was completely unable to let his mind make those free associations that are the essence of psychoanalysis. (His brain seizes on ideas and works in an entirely different way.) He was told he was unsuited for this field!

> Don't feel chained to conventional careers or conventional ways of coping. Give yourself permission to be yourself. Give up trying to be the person you always thought you should be—the model student or organized executive, for example—and let yourself be who you are.
>
> —Edward Hallowell, M.D. and John Ratey, M.D.,
> *Driven to Distraction*

Naturally, the news was a huge blow. Dr. Ratey had to get over his disappointment and come up with a new career goal. Eventually, he shifted to his specialty of neuropsychiatry, where he has made tremendous contributions, such as identifying AD/HD in adults, a real break from the traditional view of a particular patient population. He pioneered the effort to get this diagnosis accepted by mental health professionals.

Jack set out to be a physicist. He showed great promise and spent much of his early life dreaming of someday winning a Nobel Prize for science. Unfortunately, college turned out to be much tougher for him than anyone would have imagined. Although he tried his hardest, for many years, to follow this rigorous academic path, he experienced greater and greater frustration as a result of his problems with writing, organizing his research, and keeping on track when there were so many exciting projects to think up and try out. Each semester he would start out strong, but by the middle of the semester he would be far behind in his classes. Jack refused to reexamine or readjust his plan, even though it began to wear him down year after year, taking a major toll on his relationships, finances, physical health, and self-esteem. He ignored all the signals that he should shift to a different vision for his life, one that might bring him satisfaction and success.

One summer, to support himself in his long college career, he became involved in a new project being developed by the local hands-on science museum for children. It turned out that Jack was a gifted teacher; not only did the children and the other adults whom he dazzled love his shows, Jack derived a great deal of satisfaction from this work. He used his creativity and inventiveness to design incredible experiments that taught children and adults to experience physics in their everyday life. He won community service awards for this work. Job offers started to come in. It took Jack a long time to mourn and accept the fact that he was probably more suited to being a teacher than a physicist. Through this process he eventually was able to leave academia and make a meaningful contribution through a state education project geared toward motivating children to become scientists.

Finding Your Unique Zone

Once you have constructed your new vision, you will gradually begin to act on it. I'm not necessarily talking about performance and results but rather about finding what I call your unique zone: In this zone you not only are feeling comfortable with yourself and your differences, but are expressing and showing yourself and your differences. You will also be experimenting and experiencing the enjoyment of your differences—maybe for the first time in your life.

Most young adults go through an experimental period when choosing careers or making life choices. At that time in life, an individual will usually try on certain roles and identities based on his or her talents and abilities. A young man with a facility for music, for example, may join a rock band, entertain dreams of fame, and wear clothes and fashions that express this part of himself. Sometimes his ambitions will be a little too grandiose. So the young would-be rock star, based on trial and error, may eventually decide to go to college, get a degree, and teach music for a living. Whatever the outcome, the importance of this trial and error stage is that it should provide an individual with the experience and information necessary to make good decisions.

As we have seen, many adults diagnosed with AD/HD late in life do not always get the chance to complete this experimental stage. In their youth, they were not receiving the correct feedback on which way to act. Now, however, they can, in a sense, make a return trip to this time in their lives, to try on new identities. And now they are equipped with a new vision of themselves based on a more complete self-concept than they have ever possessed. This often means that their experiments will more likely lead to success.

Don Finds His Unique Zone

When Don began to act on his new vision, he started attending poetry readings, began to write poetry, and even joined a writing workshop where, after a few months, he gained the courage to show his work to the group. The group liked his work very much and even asked him to participate in a reading that the group hosted once a month.

But, as I said, the unique zone is not always about performance. One day in therapy Don lifted his pants legs and flashed his very red socks at me. "I never used to wear colors," he said. For a man who had done nothing but wear the most conservative clothes for years, red socks were rather scandalous—a fun way to confirm to himself and others who he was becoming. They signified that he was ready to let his true nature be seen, that he was no longer content to melt into the crowd, trying to "pass for normal," as Andrea Little, an AD/HD consultant, puts it.

Don had found his unique zone. Not only was he more comfortable with his differences, he was beginning to act on them, express them, and share them with others. As a result, Don's social circle widened. Because he was now less vulnerable, he shared his artistic side not just with those who might understand him and his AD/HD. He also began to reach out to a few of his colleagues at work and was surprised to find a couple of people who actually shared some of his interests but who had kept their interests to themselves. For someone who had decided to stay in his line of work, these new connections were important.

BETH FINDS HER UNIQUE ZONE

Like Don, Beth took small steps at first. She decided to take a course in graphic design at her local community college. The teacher of the course praised her work and steered her to programs where she could develop her talents. Beth also volunteered to do the graphic design for a local nonprofit arts center. Since it was not a paying job, she felt more comfortable and less pressured and was able to get the organizational support she needed in order to focus on her strengths. At the same time, she had begun hanging art in her apartment and spending more time with friends who were themselves artists or interested in art. She too had found her unique zone and wanted to share her interests with those around her.

How Do You Know When You're in
Your Unique Zone?

When Don dares to wear his red socks, or when he talks about his poetry awards, when Jennifer remembers the way she used to sing in chorus, they are contacting that place inside them where that spark still lives. In treatment, in groups or alone, the task is to pause on this feeling—this moment—and bring it into focus, enlarge it, explore it. Whether working with a professional or on your own, in order to keep moving through a successful journey, you must begin to notice those moments.

The Return of Vitality

Even after adults with AD/HD work their way through all the layers of adjusting their biochemistry, expanding their self-image—which takes a long time and requires a great deal of new data and experiences—they need to reach for a treatment goal that sets the bar higher than the absence of depression. This goal is about the recovery of something deeper: new excitement, a vitality that comes with renewed meaning and purpose or a feeling of being themselves again.

This is a critical marker I have come to look for at the end of Journey Two. When you start to feel that return of excitement and vitality, you are on the way to resolving this identity crisis and resurrecting your authentic sense of self.

In the next chapter, the focus is on utilizing this new vitality and sense of self in the most productive way. You can

I have often thought that the best way to define a man's character would be to seek out the particular mental or moral attitude in which, when it came upon him, he felt himself most deeply and intensely alive. At such moments there is a voice inside which speaks and says: "This is the real me!"

—William James in a letter to his wife, 1878

now move into the future, as opposed to remaining stuck, because you have dared to dream again. You have dared to risk the pain of reawakening old dreams and deep yearnings. You can move into the future with a sense of purpose and passion, and with a revitalized spirit.

Explorations

Taking Your Vitality Pulse

Notice those moments when you really feel alive, when your voice is a little brighter, when you smile or respond from deep inside. Find that place where you feel a certain thrill, excitement, where something touches you.

- **Hold the feeling longer than usual; notice it.**

- **Where or when have you felt it before?**

- **Pay attention when you experience this feeling. What did it feel like?**

- **What was happening when you felt it?**

- **What can you connect it to?**

The Core Meaning of Your Dreams

What were the components of your past dream that made it important to you?

- **Did your dream reflect certain values that are important to you? If so, which ones?**

- **Did it reflect your talents and abilities? If so, which ones?**

- **What part of the real you did it express?
  Does it still express that?**

Mental Mentors

A mental mentor may help you visualize a future, especially
if it's someone who also has had to overcome difficulties or
shift paths. Your role model could be someone you don't
know, like Carville or Ratey or a public figure in history or
current events, or someone in your own life.

You need to select a person who can excite your sense
of possibilities, who inspires you to help you transition into
your future vision. I call such individuals mental mentors
because you can identify with them, connect with them,
read about or hear them. Your mental mentor doesn't have
to have AD/HD or be an expert in the AD/HD field; your
mental mentor could be anyone who has faced personal
challenges and has abilities and strengths that you consider
courageous, even if in a quiet way. When you are trying to figure out a course of action or a future direction,
ask yourself what your mental mentor would do in this
situation.

- **Figure out what personal qualities of
  yours you would most like your mental
  mentor to discover or recognize. These
  are clues to what you may need to or
  want to develop.**

If you think about the qualities you respect in these
people, you may also find what it is you want to reawaken
inside of yourself.

- **What is the core meaning of your dreams?**

- **Which parts of your original dreams do you want to keep?**

- **Which are you willing to discard?**

- **Which might be reshaped to update your dreams?**

- **What is most important for you to bring with you into the future?**

- **Do you need support in order to realize your dreams?**

- **Do you need more training?**

- **Does your dream figure into your life now? If so, how?**

- **What dream do you want to reawaken that you have been secretly harboring or nurturing?**

- **What negative comments do you hear as soon as you even think about this dream? It's a luxury, it's grandiose, it's childish, it's unrealistic?**

- **When did you bury this dream?**

- **Did the derailment have anything to do with your AD/HD?**

- **What can you do about that now?**

Where Would You Like to Go?

Write a short description that captures the
true essence of how you would like your life to look in each of these areas

Relationship
Communication
Connection

Health
Self-care
Recreation
Relaxation

Operating
Your Brain

Medications

Education

Vision
More of Yourself
Authentic
Vitality
Strengths
Personal Power
Reawakened Dream

Decision
Making

Values

Your Own Strong
Inner Voice

Organization
Time
Money
"Stuff"

New Dreams
Work
School
Personal Growth

Moods
Self-esteem
Self-talk
Acceptance

Road Maps

At the RENEWAL (Rest, Education, Networking, for
Women with AD/HD Lives) workshops I give with coach
and therapist Hope Langner, one of the highlights is an ac-

tivity, developed by Hope, where the participants make beautiful collages representing their authentic future visions. You can do the same. Begin by referring to the accompanying figure. Then make a collage (or a picture) representing each of the areas listed in the figure. You can also write a brief description of each of these areas.

To expand on this exercise, pick one of the areas and develop an action plan by answering the following questions:

- **What vision of yourself or aspect of your life excites and speaks to the "real you"?**

- **What would you have to do to begin the process of developing that picture?**

- **What would be difficult about doing this? What internal barriers might prevent you from taking action?**

- **What personal strengths could you use to help you with this?**

- **What new support could you put in place to help you with this?**

- **What new external structure could you put in place to help you with this?**

- **What is the first small step you can take toward creating this picture? When will you take it?**

- **What will you do if you get stuck? (If you need help with this, keep reading.)**

Here's what you need to do if you get stuck:

- **Plan a first step—the smallest first step you can. For instance, call someone for information, or look it up on-line. (A step that may seem small may not actually be small enough if you're having trouble taking it.)**

- **If that's more than you're ready to do, start by looking up the number or even just find the phone book under the pile of stuff!**

Next, ask yourself:

- **What would be hard about taking this first step?**

- **What would prevent me from taking it? Is it the fear of being overwhelmed or of increased pressure?**

- **What would actually happen if I did take this step?**

- **What personal strengths of mine would help me take it?**

Tell your plan to one person who can envision your being able to accomplish it. Keep checking in from time to time and confide to this person any fears or resistance you may be experiencing. Remember that this individual is not there to judge your performance, but to help you stay focused on the excitement and meaning of your quest.

Crisis of Success—Focus: Your "Self" in the World

7

Protecting Your "Self" in the World

YOUR GROWING COMFORT and willingness to share yourself and your differences is a road sign that indicates that you have completed Journey Two and begun confronting the issues that characterize Journey Three. The focus now shifts from the self to the self in the world and in relationships.

I call this journey the Crisis of Success because of the personal upheaval that tends to result from having an abundance, rather than a scarcity, of options. The key to resolving this crisis is to learn to make choices based on an updated set of criteria established around what you need and value. Your "organizing style" moves to more internal methods as you begin to set boundaries. Your goal is to get off the roller coaster and learn to set boundaries as well as connect to others.

Whereas Journey Two was about expanding your self-concept and feeling comfortable with your differences, Journey Three is about learning to take care of and protect your authentic self so that you can share it with others without sacrificing the vitality, the newly awakened dreams, sense of meaning, and authenticity you have worked so long and hard to achieve. In the last part of Journey Three your

> *He threw himself on his horse and rode off in all directions.*
> —Miguel Cervantes, *Don Quixote*

challenge will be the continuing struggle to communicate to others about your differences and needs, while respecting theirs. At this point you move from letting yourself be seen to letting yourself be *known* by others and to discovering that differences are not the enemy of intimacy; when revealed and shared, differences really are a way to enrich your relationships. You will learn to protect your differences, then to give them to people as a gift of yourself.

As you move even farther, the challenge is to confront the remaining psychological barriers that may be preventing you from taking the necessary steps to make your life work—even though you feel entitled to make it work and even though you know how to do it. You may need professional support to meet this challenge. You may also need a combination of coaching and counseling to continue to support your progress.

It is easy for adults with AD/HD to misinterpret the overwhelming experiences of this new success. They commonly point to piles of new ideas and projects as evidence that they haven't made any progress at all. They can become very discouraged and believe that they have returned to their prediagnosis problems. But this stage is very different. To illustrate, I like to use the following analogy: Consider an individual who has just inherited a million dollars and is having a great deal of difficulty learning how to manage this windfall, versus someone who is having trouble managing finances because there's too little money to meet basic needs. Both situations are stressful and require tools and skills, but they represent vastly different challenges and outcomes.

As we will see in this chapter, being overwhelmed by success is not at all the same as being mired in feelings of inadequacy. These new demands on your time and energy are more representative of the true self you've wanted to express. It's important for you to know that this is a natural stage in your healthy development as an adult with AD/HD. If you expect, recognize, and understand this phase, you won't be as likely to fear that you are losing all the progress you've made. You will need to know how to navigate this stage so that eventually you can emerge from the confusion to go on to achieve a more comfortable balance.

Don's Life Spins Out of Control

By the end of Journey Two, Don had joined a poetry group and had just begun to enjoy real recognition for his talents as a poet. Not only had he shared his poetry with the group, but he had also been invited to read his poems at a poetry festival sponsored by his poetry group. He was comfortable with his differences and was even expressing them, wearing less conservative clothes and seeking out and meeting colleagues at his insurance company who shared his interests and tastes.

This was a great time for Don, and he was riding high on success until something strange and rather unexpected happened to him. After a few months of feeling as good about himself as he could ever remember, he gradually started to become overloaded again. It seemed as though he was either attending, giving, or organizing a poetry reading every two or three nights. He also was writing a newsletter for his group, designing flyers for it and putting them up before events. In addition, he had volunteered to mentor younger writers and lead a workshop for them once a week. As a result, Don's life once again felt out of control. He simply had too much going on at one time, and he was beginning to have serious problems with punctuality and organization. He arrived late to readings and sometimes even forgot about them. Once he even put the wrong evening and time on a flyer, so no one knew to attend the scheduled reading.

Of course, Don, having developed an accurate view of himself, was able to reflect on this and realize he shouldn't have been taking on these organizational responsibilities since organization was not one of his areas of strength. All the same, the group had asked him to organize a series of poetry readings and he had said yes, despite the fact that he knew it wasn't the best decision. Don couldn't seem to say no to any requests his poetry group made of him. Consequently, he made mistakes and disappointed people, just as he used to do years earlier before he had even been diagnosed. In addition, he found that he no longer had any time for his own writing. He arrived home in the evenings exhausted and feeling the same sort of depletion he'd felt

By the limits you set you protect the integrity of your day, energy, and spirit, the health of your relationships, the pursuits of your heart. When you violate your own boundaries or let another violate them stuffing spills out of your life.

—Anne Katherine, *Where to Draw the Line*

when he used to struggle with his paperwork. Don was not only overwhelmed but perplexed and discouraged because he felt that he had regressed. He wondered what had gone wrong. Where had he gone off track? How had this happened to him?

Difficulty Saying No

Adults in the Crisis of Success have a difficult time saying no to opportunities for a variety of reasons. In the past, they were often busy hiding their weaknesses or battling against their deficits—in Don's case, coping with his paperwork—and had no time for anything else. Now that people are suddenly asking them to do things they are good at, these adults don't know how to handle it. More important, they react to these opportunities just as someone who has been fasting reacts to food. They are hungry and will take anything that comes their way. After all, this is the first time in perhaps years that people have recognized their gifts and actually made requests. They relish this newfound success and want as much of it as they can get. It feels good. Saying no to someone asking them to do something they excel at feels wrong. So they jump at opportunities without reflecting. The way out of this, as we will see later in this chapter, is to develop criteria for making decisions based on who you are today.

Adults in the Crisis of Success also have a difficult time saying no to requests because they worry that they might disappoint people or return to their former state of invisibility. The fear of disappointing people comes from the many times most adults with AD/HD have let people down in the past—before diagnosis and after—because of their AD/HD. Perhaps they arrived late to appointments or missed an important occasion because of their poor organizational skills. As a result, the people they cared most about felt hurt and disappointed in them. For instance, long before Don had been diagnosed, he twice showed up without his poems at poetry readings organized by a close friend. He had forgotten them at home. His friend began to suspect he was doing this on purpose. Unfortunately, Don had no way of explaining his lapses at that time and felt he had no excuse. As he continued to let people down—showing up late for the class he taught, forgetting his lesson plan, leaving his students' poems at home, or even losing them in a café—he decided there was no solution but to withdraw. When he lost his teaching job he decided that he would never try to work as a teacher again. He also completely stopped giving poetry readings.

The shame he felt as a result of letting people down was partly responsible for his decision to leave poetry altogether and become an insurance salesman, an occupation and identity that, as we have seen, left him feeling invisible. The more Don withdrew from the people who mattered to him and hid behind his safe, but suffocating, identity as an insurance salesman, the more invisible he became. Soon he no longer felt he had anything exciting to give or share at all.

When asked to organize the reading series, Don feared that had he refused, the group might stop making requests of him. He would no longer be asked to read his poetry or to mentor the younger writers. Eventually, he would return to being the insurance salesman who seemed to have no other life, no gifts, and nothing much to share with others. Of course, Don's fears were irrational. When the group made this request of Don, he was already performing a number of tasks for the group and could have easily declined by simply saying he did not have time.

Ironically, the fear of disappointing people can become a self-fulfilling prophecy. If you agree to take on more requests than you can handle, for fear of letting people down, you'll end up doing exactly what you wanted to avoid. By saying no to some requests, you'll be more likely to come through for yourself and others when you do say yes to a request.

You Can't Do It All

Confusion is often a sign of the Crisis of Success. You may feel that you have come a long way and are just beginning to experience the thrill of success when you get hit in the face with what may seem like a million difficult choices and pressures. This experience will splinter your attention, and you may feel as though you are going in a dozen different directions at once. When you are confronted with the need to choose, you may not want to; you may want to have it all at once. And when you can't, you become frustrated.

Being out of control and confused, even if you are experiencing more success, can be scary. You might feel that you will never get off the roller coaster you're riding, that there will be no end to this time, which is both exhilarating and frightening. You might be scared to pass up any opportunity and, as a result, become overloaded. You might even suspect that your recent success is an accident and that failure will begin to revisit you at any moment.

Rest assured that the above are all signs that you have arrived at the Crisis of Success. If you start to take positive steps, you will emerge from this crisis and begin a smoother, easier course.

We have seen Beth develop her self-concept and get back in touch with her real passions. She understood, at this point, that her earlier choices had aggravated her AD/HD symptoms. She also understood now that her sense of identity was not based in a clean desktop but on art, design, and enjoying her friends. She returned to school in graphic design, volunteered her services as a graphic designer, and soon found herself giddy with all the success she was having. People loved her work, and she took on more and more. Beth now had three volunteer jobs as well as going to school full-time.

Once again, Beth found herself having trouble with deadlines, arriving late for classes and meetings, and feeling exhausted. But she was no longer on a treadmill because now she was truly in motion, acting on her strengths. She was on a roller coaster, being flung up and down. She also was having fun. But as the roller coaster went faster, Beth began to get tired and disoriented. She still felt out of control. Eventually, she would need to stop and get off the ride. She would want to travel a more direct and comfortable course. But just knowing that she was on the roller coaster and that this ride was natural, that it would last for a while—not forever—if she learned to make choices, comforted her and allowed her to relax and enjoy her progress (and the ride!).

JENNIFER'S OVERABUNDANCE OF ACTIVITIES

At this point in her journey, Jennifer was really exploring her identity apart from her AD/HD, and was having a great time. She had taken up yoga, enrolled in a photography class, reconnected with old friends, and volunteered her time at local charities. She had not felt so alive in years. But she still had the responsibilities of her family, and the more activities she took on outside the home, the more difficult it became for her to negotiate her two worlds. She started on the home front: forgetting to pay bills, picking her kids up from school late, and having trouble arranging occasional nights out with her husband.

But her difficulties no longer had to do with the fact that she had invested all of her identity in her ability to be a perfect non-AD/HD mother and wife. And she no longer sought escape through all-night excursions to the bus station, which had been her way of escaping her home for years. Whereas she had spent most of her life grounded entirely in her deficits, now she had started exploring areas of experience that would fulfill her. She really liked everything she was doing now: the yoga classes, the time with old friends, the volunteer work, and her life as a mother and wife at home.

However, all her projects started interfering with each other. At times she was late for yoga class or couldn't even go because of a responsibility she had taken on as a volunteer. When something went wrong with her family, she started to feel guilty, just as she had earlier. She was on a roller coaster and needed to find a way to keep the activities she enjoyed from overwhelming her. She needed to make choices for the first time in years between a number of good options that really meant something to her.

Making Good Choices

The way off the roller coaster is learning to make good choices. Now that you know what matters to you, what fulfills you, and what makes you feel most like yourself, you can develop criteria for making such choices based on self-knowledge rather than on frustration and fear. But first you must give yourself permission to say no and confront the fear that you may never have another chance, that others won't continue to include or appreciate you.

Jennifer had to figure out which organizations she would drop out of, which she would attend infrequently, and which she really wanted to make a contribution to. This was not easy; she had to dig deep to figure out what values meant the most to her. The criteria she used for deciding had to change from merely what other people wanted from her to what she valued.

Don had to come to terms with the fact that he had already taken on too much. He had to guard against taking on anything else at this point, even if it sounded great. An opportunity, no matter how impressive, that drew on his deficits and left him feeling crazed and out of control was not a good choice for him.

For everyone, making choices always has a component of loss. Saying no to something, even if it allows you to say yes to something else, is a loss of that thing you've let go. This loss may be felt more intensely by the individual with AD/HD since he or she may fear that nothing else will come along. While this feeling is to be expected, adults with AD/HD should remember that they are in a new stage of their journey now and that they have created their own opportunities through their abilities, and good opportunities most likely will continue to present themselves. They have spent so many years feeling like impostors that the expectation that they will be unmasked and everything will fall apart is a long and difficult one to change.

Journey Three

Focus:
Your Self in
the World

When adults begin to say no to opportunities, they may need to go through what I call a mini–grief cycle every time they make this choice. It may last only a few minutes, but the feeling of loss, then acceptance might be reexperienced whenever you see a friend or colleague handle or complete so many things so much more easily and quickly than you can. You may have to find a way to appreciate that what you have to offer might be different or produced in a different way in order to continually return to acceptance. Rather than focusing entirely on the speed or quantity of accomplishments, highlight the quality or complexity of your work, the uniqueness of your approach, your creativity, or what you give to others. To do this, you have to continually monitor and sort out your criteria for making decisions and remind yourself of what you value each time you make an important choice.

Lance's Case: Born to Ride

For adults like Lance, who tend to hyperfocus, multitask, and have an intense need for high stimulation, the roller coaster is nothing new. In fact, because they have always operated in their areas of strengths, they have been riding the roller coaster for most of their lives. Their problem is that they *like* the exhaustion and depletion of the roller coaster and, as we have seen, will not try to step off it until they go through a number of crashes and begin to feel the serious consequences of living out of control.

When these adults see their deficits, however, they are likely to keep riding the roller coaster, but now with a difference. By this point, these adults should, at the very least, know that, among other difficulties, they tend to overwork simply because they thrive on stimulation. In time they also see that their overwork eventually leads to chaos and crisis, and so they should be able to slow down more, at least periodically, instead of driving themselves into the ground. Those who don't come to this point remain stuck in perpetual motion.

For example, as we've seen, Lance realized that, although he would never be able to work for a large company, he needed more structure and more limits on his freedom at work. Because of his problems with executive functions (see chapter 1), he needed someone to manage him so that he could produce his unique "sound." Thomas Brown uses the metaphor of "a symphony orchestra in which each musician can play well but where there is no conductor to activate and organize the orchestra so that all can play their part of the same score on the same beat. If there is no one to signal the introduction of woodwinds, if the efforts of individual musicians are not integrated and regulated by a competent conductor, the orchestra will not produce good music."*

So when an old client for whom Lance had worked over the years offered to take Lance on in his small company and give him a lot of freedom, Lance was at the place in his journey where he was able to accept the opportunity. It was a good fit for Lance. This client loved Lance's work but also saw his deficits clearly. He knew Lance was a poor administrator and tended to take on too many projects at once. So he did not give Lance any paperwork responsibilities and limited the number of projects assigned to him. While this arrangement kept Lance off the roller coaster for a while, he got back on by spending too much time and being a perfectionist with each project. For months he produced some of the best work of his life. He, like Don, had a hard time saying no to even the most unreasonable requests of his clients, though not merely because he was afraid of saying no. Lance liked the rush he got from taking on challenges that might seem overwhelming to others. But eventually and ironically, Lance's drive depleted him, and the quality of his work suffered. In the whirl of activity, Lance hardly saw this, and once again he was heading toward disaster.

Luckily, Lance's new boss liked his work enough to intervene and was able to show him when he was veering toward a crash. He also asked that Lance get a business coach who could act as an external monitor, and Lance agreed. For adults like Lance, who sometimes have a difficult time avoiding overextending themselves, external monitoring is invaluable, and, in Lance's case, it helped him keep his job.

* Thomas Brown, "Does ADHD Diagnosis Require Impulsivity-Hyperactivity?: A Response to Gordon and Barkeley," *ADHD Report* 7, no. 6 (1999): 1–7.

At times, despite the best efforts of his coach, Lance crashed anyway and was late with projects. At other times, he delivered excellent work while maintaining a balance between work and his own well-being.

In many ways, Lance's situation was ideal. His boss was more than understanding and gave him the freedom he required. Lance got a coach when he needed one most and managed to succeed, even if it was a constant struggle. Other adults with Lance's intensity are not always so fortunate. They may find an ideal situation but fail to get the necessary external monitoring. For this reason, they have a very hard time getting off the roller coaster and can get stuck here. If you notice that you can't seem to get off the roller coaster, consider getting a coach or enlisting someone who can help you slow down when your efforts are becoming counterproductive.

Criteria for Making Decisions

Adults with AD/HD come in to see me at some point and tell me about a great offer they have just had or some new idea or project that has come their way. They feel that since this great opportunity is out there, they must act on it. They are still stuck in their old view that something good rarely comes along. They haven't readjusted their thinking to understand that there are lots of good ideas out there, lots of good offers, but that the goodness of the idea or opportunity shouldn't be the sole basis for making a decision. You have to consider a larger set of criteria that includes your family, your goals, your health, your friends, your finances, your energy level, your organizational skills, and your particular way of operating.

Ask yourself: What do you want? What do you need?

What do you value? Why are you saying yes to a particular option? Which things should you let go of? These questions may be simple, but they're not easy to answer.

As you consider these questions, keep in mind that developing criteria is not a one-time exercise. Your criteria will change, and you should change them whenever you need to. For now, you will want to carefully consider these questions and come up with answers. It's important to develop criteria for making decisions so that when you're confronted with opportunities at any given moment, you won't act on those old "starvation" tendencies and once again overload yourself.

The first step to developing new criteria is to examine your present criteria for making decisions. While it may seem that you have no criteria at all, in fact you do. Without your knowing it, the fear that you may never get another good opportunity could be one of your current criteria. This fear leads you to believe you must take every opportunity that allows you to operate in an area of strength. Another criterion of an adult in the Crisis of Success might be: "Say yes to any request so that you won't disappoint anyone." But, as we have seen, utilizing these criteria will lead to depletion.

When Don reflected on the criteria he was using to make decisions, he came up with the following list:

1. **If it is new, and in an area of strength, seriously consider doing it.**

2. **Say yes to any opportunity that has to do with poetry.**

3. **Don't say no when people make requests. They might not ask you to do anything again.**

After examining these criteria, Don understood that in some way they were counterproductive. The first one had worked a year or two ago when his main goal was expanding his self-concept and learning about his strengths. But now that he knew that his focus was poetry, this criterion no longer made sense in his life. His second criterion, while focused on something that meant a great deal to him, was too general and had led him to take on organizational tasks, such as coordinating readings, for which he was ill suited. He knew that he wanted to focus on poetry, but he would now need to do so in a more specific way. Finally, his third criterion had to do with his fear of saying no to people. Looking at this one, Don realized that he would need to work on learning to say no. He came to understand that not saying no was in fact leading him to disappoint instead of please others. He was in fact unwittingly creating the very thing he was trying to avoid.

Once he examined these criteria, none of which he had thought about before, he could revise them to reflect what he now valued most about himself. After considering all of his gifts and priorities, he decided that he wanted to take on writing and teaching opportunities that would allow him to produce more work and remain connected with other writers. With these goals in mind, he formulated the following criteria:

1.   **Take opportunities that will allow you to write more and be serious about writing.**

2.   **Take opportunities that will allow you to connect with other writers through**

mentoring.

3. **Say no to opportunities that might get in the way of 1 and 2, especially those that involve organizational tasks.**

This list helped Don stay focused: He was able to catch himself when he occasionally slipped and returned to his old criteria. Gradually, he became effective at saying no to activities that would get in the way of his own writing. He also found that his criteria simplified the decision-making process; he was now less uncertain about which opportunities to accept and which to reject. At the same time, he had more time to write, send his poems to literary magazines, give readings, and mentor other poets. He was now off the roller coaster and using his strengths in a more focused and effective way than ever before. He was also aware that his criteria would change as his life changed. So from time to time, when his life felt too busy or he seemed to be making the wrong decision, he reassessed his goals and asked himself if it was time to revise his criteria.

If you find yourself making decisions that are not in line with your criteria, ask yourself why you make these decisions. Have your values changed? If so, you probably need to change your criteria. Have you gone back to old criteria? If so, you need to review your values and priorities. Or has your life changed in a significant way? If so, your criteria may not fit anymore. Let's say, for example, that one of your children has left home for college while the others have grown older and more independent. This will mean that you have more time to devote to your career and other activities outside of your family.

Take note that your criteria will at times be in conflict

and you will need to figure out how to negotiate these conflicts. Also make sure that your criteria are realistic. You may decide to get some support—professional or otherwise—in order to avoid overload.

"You Can Do Anything, You Just Can't Do Everything"

I came across the above line in a magazine article in which prominent people revealed their secrets for success. When my clients who are in Journey Three begin new projects or arrive at a new level of success or satisfaction in life, they too find that they must often figure out what to let go of and what to say yes to.

By gaining an awareness of what this crisis is about and taking on the new challenge of making good choices, you will eventually get off the roller coaster and begin to focus on your strengths in a more effective way than ever before. Without the kind of decision-making process that I describe here, your planners and AD/HD medication may not bring you lasting results. In the next chapter we'll continue this discussion of how to organize our lives from within.

Explorations

Roller Coaster or Treadmill?

If you are unsure whether you are in the Crisis of Success, you may need to determine whether you're on the roller coaster or the treadmill. Keep in mind that the depletion of the roller coaster feels different from the depletion of the treadmill. If you are overwhelmed by your strengths, you will derive satisfaction from the activities that are over-whelming you. To confirm that you are on the roller coaster, ask yourself these two simple questions:

- **Are you working more in your areas of strength?**

- **Are your activities meaningful to you?**

Examining Your Current Criteria

- **What are your current criteria for making decisions?**

- **Are any of these criteria too broad or counterproductive?**

- **If so, do you need to update them or give them up completely?**

- **What feelings are you aware of when thinking of giving them up?**

- **What will it mean for you to change your criteria?**

- **What do you want?**

- **What do you need?**

- **What do you value?**

8

Organizing Your "Self"
in the World

IN THIS CHAPTER, we will look at effective ways of organizing your life so that you can continue to protect yourself from distraction and detours that might keep you out of your unique zone and move you away from yourself.

When most people think of organizing, they think of Post-it notes, folders, files, and other tools for classifying and ordering things. (These types of tools are what I call external aids.) However, as we have seen, you can also take an approach to organizing that starts from the inside and develops out of your values and knowledge of self.

When I talk about expanding the idea of organization beyond externals, adults who are just starting their journeys are often afraid that I am telling them to give up and live in clutter. They ask me questions like "Don't you think organizing your work space is a useful goal?" My answer is yes, of course. However, too many adults with AD/HD make the most basic form of organization the yardstick by which they measure their worth, making it the gold standard by which they decide if they're entitled to have a life.

External aids become much more effective once you begin to organize from within. So I encourage you to keep

> For whatever purpose you were put on this planet, it couldn't be to organize clutter.
>
> —B. Sher, *Live the Life You Love*

using them; just don't forget that organization is not just about files, date books, and systems. It is finally about who you are and what you value in life. This will affect your ability to organize in an increasingly satisfying way (even if your piles never completely go away!)

Moving from Personal Planners to Personal Power

Often the approach to organizational difficulties is not connected to a sense of meaning or inner drive. For adults with AD/HD, for whom a high degree of engagement is usually necessary for the completion of tasks, this link is crucial. You need to make sure your schedule contains places you *want* to go and things you *want* to do; otherwise you won't keep to your schedule very long, no matter how hard you try.

The process of advancing through the organizational hierarchy is somewhat organic. In other words, your developing self-concept will not only allow you but also require you to do this. So if you are having difficulty organizing from within, don't put pressure on yourself. Have patience and allow yourself to undergo this process at your own pace. Here it is in a nutshell:

In Journey One, you

- **depend mostly on externals such as paper aids, beepers, buzzers, and personal planners;**

- **work mostly alone.**

In Journey Two, you

- enlist the support of others—professionals as well as some friends and family;

- let people get closer to you in order to provide support.

In Journey Three,

- internal organization brings an increased sense of control and choice;

- you are able to respond to your inner signals, your own internal voice that tells you what to do in your own best interest, rather than being pulled by outside forces and demands as much;

- better internal organization indirectly leads to better external organization.

For a detailed chart, see the "Aids for Organizing Your Life" in appendix A

Organizing Around Meaning

In *First Things First*, Stephen R. Covey uses the metaphor of filling a jar with rocks, pebbles, and sand to explain how to organize effectively. He points out that if you start with sand and pebbles, you won't be able to fit the big rocks in the jar. But if you put in the big rocks first, you can fit the pebbles around them. He means, of course, that if you don't put what's important in place first, your life will fill up with lesser priorities and activities. This is what I mean when I talk about organizing around meaning. In the preceding chapter we saw what happens when you have too many big rocks. Now we will look at the importance of having enough big rocks. Without them, you may become confused about what to do and get lost in a sea of meaningless activities, spending many frustrating hours trying to figure out what to focus on because nothing in particular stands out and compels you.

Covey's metaphor is especially apt for adults with AD/HD, who often have what feels like a million things to do and, instead of prioritizing, try to respond to all of them. They often feel that if they first do what is most important, they will never get to the little things. As a result, they are overwhelmed by pebbles and sand and never get to their big rocks. For it is the small things that eat up much of their time and which are often the very activities that they struggle with the most. Anyone who spends a great deal of time and energy doing things that are especially difficult for them will become depleted and lose vitality and confidence.

Though it may seem counterintuitive to you, organizing your schedule around activities that you deem meaningful and important will result in a better structure around which to put the smaller tasks. Another positive outcome is that you will feel less depleted and more competent. Having struggled to feel entitled to focus on meaningful activities, you are now faced with the challenge of learning to let them anchor your life.

To start meeting this challenge, here's what you need to do: Think of one activity that you find entertaining or engaging and that has in the past lured you away from your daily schedule. Make this activity the centerpiece of your day and fill in your schedule around it. By making this activity your priority, you will avoid feeling guilty and be more likely to stick to your schedule. You will also be on your way to building a structure that will reaffirm who you are as a person, build your confidence and vitality, and, as a result, allow you to accomplish smaller, frustrating tasks more easily.

If It's Thursday, It Must Be Toilets

Jennifer asked me why she couldn't keep to her schedule for cleaning her house. Repeatedly she failed to fulfill her priority for Thursday, which, according to her schedule, was cleaning toilets. While this may seem to be no big deal, it really frustrated her. What she needed to see was that she had let cleaning toilets shape her Thursdays, thereby dooming herself to failure. How would it feel to wake up to a day that was first and foremost about cleaning toilets? What she needed to do was shape her Thursdays around an activity that was really important to her and that would motivate her to take the few minutes to clean toilets so that she could move on to this activity.

How Meaning Creates Order

Beth had been trying for almost a year to clear out and organize her spare room without any clear idea of what she wanted to do with this space. But when she became a student in graphic design, she needed a computer, and the room became the perfect place for her computer and much of her schoolwork. Within a day of purchasing the computer, Beth had set up and organized her spare room—which had been a mess and a source of unhappiness for years—to accommodate her computer. She was able to accomplish her task so quickly because she could picture how the room was to be used. While the room was never perfectly organized, it never approached the chaos

THE TRUE MEANING OF DISCIPLINE

When adults with AD/HD come up against the wall of schedules they cannot meet, files they cannot organize, rooms they cannot seem to clean, they redouble their efforts and tell themselves to be more disciplined. But what do they mean by the word *discipline*? Many adults with AD/HD think of discipline as a way of motivating themselves with harshness and punitive consequences. Doing that, however only makes us end up feeling bad about ourselves, blaming ourselves, and feeling disappointed. That's the last thing adults with AD/HD need.

In fact, the word *discipline* comes from the word *disciple*, which means "to follow with love." In this sense of the word, you do need more discipline—more connectedness and engagement—in order to keep to your schedule. But without true engagement in your life, you will not have the stimulation or energy to accomplish what is most difficult for you.

that had engulfed it when it had no meaning or purpose in Beth's life.

If your schedule or your organizational goal has no real meaning to you, not only do you stay disorganized despite getting treatment for AD/HD, you also become demoralized, as you continually blame yourself for breaking your schedule or falling short of your goal.

Mary Crouch, a professional organizer, helps each of her clients transform a room in their home into a sanctuary, a place that reflects who they are or who they are becoming. She sees organizing as one means of getting at your true self and your home as a place that supports meaning in your life, where you're surrounded by the things you love or that hold special meaning for you.

Knowing How to Operate Your Brain

To organize your life more effectively, you must know how your particular brain works. While this understanding may include some of the general information you learned after diagnosis and early treatment about brain chemistry, and how medication affects it, every individual's brain functions differently. Many adults never really notice this fact. They don't have to. They simply live life on automatic pilot, so to speak. However, adults with AD/HD need to be especially aware of the conditions under which they function best.

A large part of organizing your life involves getting to know how and when your specific brain operates well and when it doesn't. As you become more acquainted with your brain, you will be able to adjust or organize your environment so that you can function at a higher level. To do this, you will need to become aware of both the conditions around you as well as your own response to them at any given time. This knowledge will also be necessary for the later stages of Journey Three, when you begin focusing on effectively communicating your needs to others. Obviously, if you don't know yourself well, you won't be able to tell others what you require in order to operate well.

In this section we'll look at six variables that must be considered and balanced when exploring how your brain works. As clinical psychologist Harriet Lerner says in her book *The Dance of Intimacy*, your goal is to organize your life to support "who you are really, not what you'd like to be."

You must make careful observations long before you even attempt this. Wait until a day when things are going well and when you are operating well: Your mood is good, your energy level is high, and you are thinking well. Then figure out what is different about this day—or these few hours if that's what it is. Your answers will be unique to you, such as, "Oh yeah, the kids were out of the house for an

hour when I cooked dinner," or "I went to the park for a short walk before I came home after work."

Once you've analyzed the variables that affect how your mind works, your next step is to balance these variables in order to keep your brain and your life running more smoothly. I call this balancing act the Tightrope Effect. You won't be able to create and maintain a balance all the time, but you will feel more of a sense of control. When one variable increases or decreases, other variables will have to be adjusted. You'll need to assess the situation and remix the variables in a way that will allow you to operate at your best. Remember, the point of all this is not to operate as you *think* you should operate or to catch yourself when you're not operating well, but to know when and how you operate well and not well.

Although how you operate is unique to you, it will be helpful for you to consider the following variables when you begin thinking about when and why you do or do not function at your best, as well as what to modify and adjust.

1. STIMULATION/STRESS CONTINUUM

Understanding the relationship between stress and stimulation is critical if you are to maintain your sense of balance. Several years ago I heard Dr. John Ratey, coauthor of *Driven to Distraction*, warn the audience at an AD/HD conference that adults should be careful not to reduce good stimulation in an effort to reduce stress. He suggested that this strategy was a mistake for adults with AD/HD, who often need the right kind of stimulation to stay interested and alert.

I too have noticed that reducing stimulation can actually create more stress in the lives of my clients. This is because without good stimulation, the lives of adults with AD/HD often lack meaning, excitement, structure, and focus. Consequently they feel more stress, accomplish less, and become more depressed and less engaged with the world in general.

To illustrate how to create a balance between stimulation and stress, let's use the metaphor of the tightrope. Good stimulation gives you enough force to keep you balanced as you walk the tightrope. Without enough good stimulation, you will become *underwhelmed* and lose your balance. On the other hand, like a strong wind, too much stimulation—good or bad—can knock you off the rope. Constantly observing and readjusting the kind and amount of stimulation you're receiving is key. Of course, only you can determine what sort of stimulation is good and how much of it you need in order to keep yourself balanced.

2. STRUCTURE

Structure comprises boundaries, limits, and conditions—all of which may be determined by other people or by deadlines. Structure is an external framework that defines what you're doing and may dictate the timing of an activity or the location where it takes place.

Most people, especially those with AD/HD, function better with structure. But this can be tricky, because adults with AD/HD need structure *and* a lack of structure. Too much structure will not allow them the independence and space for creativity that many adults with AD/HD thrive on. Too little structure may leave the adult with AD/HD drowning in a sea of freedom. So you will need to find out how much structure and freedom you need. If you are following a program laid out by others, make sure the structure allows you the flexibility and room for creativity you require. As with stimulation and stress, you will need to experiment with structure and freedom in order to find a comfortable balance for you.

3. Support

Support provides the help you need in your areas of deficits or even, if need be, your areas of strengths. You may require support on a daily basis or on a project-by-project basis or simply when you feel out of control. Support is especially helpful when you feel you are not in control of the variables we are discussing here. By this point, you should be able to use support (helping with external organization, household help, or academic help; the services of a secretary, bookkeeper, coach, or counselor, to name a few possibilities) more effectively. The key is knowing when you need support, how much support to use, in which areas, and when to adjust your levels of support.

Supporters need to be accepting and have as their goal to have you become more yourself, not just to keep your nose to the grindstone. You must come away feeling replenished and refreshed, not just organized.

4. Speed: Pace or Spacing of Activities

Everyone needs some transition time between activities. You may need a lot of recovery and relaxation time between projects, or you may recover more quickly. Some thrive on multitasking and do better juggling a number of activities in the air at the same time. In cases where pace or spacing is predetermined, you will have to adjust other variables to balance this out.

·

5. DEGREE OF DIFFICULTY

Before you undertake tasks, consider their degree of difficulty: What intellectual, physical, manual, or emotional demands will they make on you? Try to anticipate the quality or quantity of time and effort you will need to invest. For some, a particular task might require little focusing; for others it may require a lot.

6. DEGREE OF CONTROL

At any given time, there are always some elements in your life that you have less control over than you would like. This is when you have to adjust the elements you *can* control in order to keep your balance. Often this adjustment will affect other people; in the next chapter you will sharpen your communication skills to help smooth out any potential frictions.

Whenever you can't adjust any element of a task or situation, you have to change your view or mental state. Acknowledge that you're in for a rough patch and expect it, knowing it will pass. There are very few situations where you can't exert some control, at least in your attitude.

REMIXING THE VARIABLES

To evaluate tasks and projects according to the above variables, you should keep in mind that these variables are interrelated. Let's say a particular task has a high degree of difficulty and you don't have control over your environment, which has many distractions and in which you would have a hard time focusing. You may need to increase the level of support or reduce the pace or difficulty of the task. Once you see how they work together for you, you can be-

> The AD/HD brain is like a Stradivarius, a delicate instrument capable of producing beautiful sounds under the right conditions. You must take time to care for it, protect and tune it, and learn to play it well.

gin remixing these variables whenever necessary. For example, if for one week you are losing support or structure (perhaps your coach or someone you work with closely is sick or on vacation), you might find it helps to take on projects that require less attention or have fewer variables. On the other hand, you might decide to increase the interesting stimulation to keep you focused.

Once you get a feel for how you operate, you will have another tool that will help you make good decisions. When you learn how to remix the variables that are most crucial for you, you can begin to assess situations and make powerful decisions. Before, when you were confronted with difficult situations, you might have said something like: "It looks like I'll just have to go through hell for the next week/month/six months." Now, you might say to yourself: "Next week may be very stressful. I have a report due, and I'm coming down with a cold and my family is coming into town. I will need more support."

This kind of decision-making power will also allow you to develop your priorities and stick with them so you can avoid the sort of overload that we discussed in the previous chapter. For example, when I started giving presentations at conferences many years ago, I knew that public speaking was an activity that required a great deal of preparation for me. Therefore, I commonly said no to extra activities at conferences in order to get the kind of rest and focus I needed. But my needs changed later when I had gained experience speaking in public and so required less mental preparation for presentations. At that point, I made it my priority to say yes to nourishing activities that involve relationships and connecting and that actually give me more energy and enthusiasm to do a good job. You, too, need to reassess your priorities and needs from time to time and, if they change, remix the variables to regain your balance.

Here is another example of how you might adjust operating the variables to function at your best. You have a big project due. Relatives from out of town just called and asked to come and stay with you for a week.

First, assess the situation and note your possible responses. Let's say you don't like these people, don't know them well, or they only want to see you to save the price of a hotel room while they tour the city where you live. You could just say no.

On the other hand, maybe you haven't seen your aunt and uncle in twenty years; they live in Italy, are eighty years old, and you'll probably never see them again. In that case you might decide that their visit is more important to you than your project, and insist that they stay with you and ask for an extension at work.

More likely, the situation falls somewhere in the middle, and you feel torn. You really like these relatives, whom you see once a year. You don't want to miss the chance to spend time with them. But you know you are going to have a rough time because of your project deadline. This would be tough for anyone, but having AD/HD makes this situation particularly difficult.

You could say yes under certain conditions—they stay at a hotel, and you split the cost. Or you might make it clear in advance how much time you'll have available to spend with them. You also might consider getting more support; for instance, you might ask your mother-in-law to watch the children or even for her to keep them overnight during part of the visit.

You could consider increasing your structure at work during the week before they arrive to help you keep focused on the project. You might get a coworker to give you some informal coaching—to encourage you to stay on a schedule and meet your deadline.

Most important, you need to look very closely at your choices and understand why you are making them. Think about the stress level of the visit so that you know what you are saying yes to. Think about whether you are saying yes because it is too difficult to say no. Once you know what the implications of your decisions are, move on to thinking about how to remix and adjust the variables, to operate at your best during the visit.

The Intersection of AD/HD and Psychology

Until now, we have focused on how you can protect yourself in order to live in your unique zone and avoid depletion. But protection alone is not enough to establish healthy and fulfilling personal and professional relationships with others. So it is important that adults not get stuck merely protecting themselves, which leads to isolation. Your next task is learning to protect yourself while you connect with others. To do this, you will need to confront psychological barriers that arise where getting your AD/HD needs met intersects with your personal and interpersonal barriers.

Explorations

Think of a difficult situation from your own life where you feel or have felt out of control or out of balance. Use the list below to think through how you would need to adjust or remix the variables to make it work for the way you operate.

- **Stimulation stress continuum**

- **Structure**

- **Support**

- **Speed—pace or spacing of activities**

- **Degree of difficulty (intellectual, physical, manual, or emotional)**

- **Degree of control**

- **Distractions in the environment**

- **Other responsibilities**

- **Here are some possible responses**

- **Cutting down**

- **Cutting out**

- **Sharing tasks**

- **Delegating tasks**

- **Modifying your environment**

Also consider the variables that relate to your physical well-being, and make adjustments as necessary.

- **Energy level**

- **Hormonal fluctuations**

- **Medication**

- **Physical response to stress**

- **Rest**

- **Diet**

- **Exercise**

Write a couple of plans for handling this difficult situation. Don't worry for now about the interpersonal level; focus instead on the variables by:

- **Looking at your weekly schedule.**

- **Determining whether the choices contain any of the following elements:**

  - **A sense of meaning or value**

  - **Rewards or fulfillment**

  - **Stimulation, excitement**

  - **A sense of connection**

- **Naming your "big rocks" and working in everything else around them.**

- **Observing when things are going well so you can set up things more like that situation.**

9

ADDing Connection to Protection

AT THIS POINT YOU ARE ABLE to start "giving" to others the unique self you have come to value and live comfortably with, while retaining the sense of authenticity and uniqueness you've worked so long to achieve and protect. But when you begin this process of letting yourself be known to others, you may come up against deep, unconscious fears, especially when dealing with the people closest to you.

"One thing that's really challenging about living with an invisible disability," says Hope Langner, a therapist and coach, "is always having to say the hard thing out loud, whether that's asking for help, explaining why you cannot or will not do something, explaining your unique thinking process or something else that is unexpected."*

Protection/Connection Dilemma

One summer, I gave myself a birthday present of a two-month writer's retreat in a beautiful part of New England. I

*Hope Langner, "ADD: An Invisible Disability," *ADDvance: A Magazine for Women with Attention Deficit Disorder*, July–August 2000, p. 5.

lived in a small cottage out in the country, on a beautiful piece of land in an idyllic setting where I wrote. Even though I had rented my own cottage, I was living on the same property with its owners, a wonderful retired couple. I was happy for their closeness and enjoyed their company. At the same time, though, I was there for a limited time to write. I knew by that point how I operate, and how delicate my attention is.

The challenge I had to confront was how to continue to protect my own needs and limited time while also developing a close relationship with these people. Such special circumstances required that I examine this dynamic in depth. A couple of times each day there would be a phone call, a wave from the deck, or a knock on the door with some kind of nice invitation. I frequently needed to find a way to say *no* without sounding as if I didn't want their company. I couldn't pretend I wasn't home. I couldn't refuse to answer the phone. I couldn't pretend there were other things to do, other places to go, or other people to see. I couldn't shove the issue under my mental piles and focus elsewhere. There was no running away from this issue—this was a stark and frightening reality for me.

Somehow I would have to discuss my differences in a way that didn't sound apologetic or false or ridiculous. I had to somehow explain my rather extreme need for focus. Whereas other people could take more breaks and shifts without losing theirs, I needed to guard against being interrupted. I knew it would be hard for them to understand me. Intensifying my dilemma was the fact that as much as I wanted to write and stay focused, I also desired the pleasure of developing this potentially deep and satisfying relationship.

The Protected and Connected Self

When I returned home after my summer in New England and shared this dilemma with my clients, they immediately related to it. Over time, I realized that to resolve a dilemma of this sort, one must learn how to navigate what I call the "protection/connection continuum."

We have talked about the importance of knowing how to protect your self and your uniqueness and knowing how to make your life work for you. But protecting yourself should be done in a healthy way, rather than defensively. Otherwise, you may find yourself feeling lonely, with few meaningful and satisfying relationships.

Even when you know how you operate and what your needs are, you might still enter into a relationship or a situation where you forget all about your own needs and focus on what the group demands or what an individual close to you needs. In this case, you would be too far over on the connect side of the continuum. If you spend too much time on the connect side, you will become overwhelmed and may feel out of control or angry or resentful or depleted. As a result, at some point you might decide that relationships take too much of a toll on you and wind up too far on the protect side, feeling isolated and depleted.

We all need to protect ourselves, but it should be in a way that actually promotes relationships rather than moves us away from them. Boundaries and limits are the protective devices for everyone, not just those with AD/HD, that make us feel safe in relationships so we can be intimate and close without getting swallowed up and disappearing.

By this point in your development, you will no longer feel that you "deserve" to be mistreated in relationships or

Look at the parts of your life that work that have integrity. This wholeness comes from the limits you have set to protect them. Any part of your life that is not working can be improved by boundaries. Whether the organism is you, your body, your health, a friendship, your marriage, your work or your energy, its integrity can be strengthened by boundaries.

—Anne Katherine,
Where to Draw the Line

even that you need to hide your true self or withdraw. However, you may be surprised to find, even at this advanced stage, that at times you are unable or afraid to share your needs and differences with others.

Family Barriers to Connection—Rules, Roles, and "Change-Back" Messages

Family dynamics play a major role in all families when someone changes, even in a healthy family. This has little or nothing to do with whether the person who is changing has AD/HD. But often when an individual with AD/HD is on medication and growing in ways we have described so far, she will feel a new power, become more assertive, and begin to stake out a claim to new territory, either physical or emotional, which she may have been too overwhelmed to do previously. She will set new limits, new boundaries, which may feel like a loss to other important people in her life—or may require other people to rearrange their behavior or lives. This altered dynamic is always uncomfortable in families and it takes time and support for family members to adjust to a new way of relating to one another.

The kind of changes that an adult with AD/HD might begin to make at this stage can sometimes upset the way the family has been operating. Such changes might upset the roles that people in the family have been playing comfortably or break sacred traditions and unspoken rules that have been operating unchallenged for years, even for generations, in a family, affecting the culture of the extended family. It is no surprise, then, that these changes would be strongly resisted by family members. This backlash could threaten to undermine the process of the person with AD/HD.

The family might send out what are called in the field of family systems "change-back messages." These overt and subtle messages can hook you and stop you in powerful ways. Change-back messages are unconscious cues from others that tell adults who have broken out of old roles and behaviors to return to their familiar ways. Families, for better or worse, operate with a strong pull to return to familiar ways of interacting. It is important for you to understand that eventually, if you resist these messages, you will all move to a more healthy way of relating and living together.

Psychological Barriers to Communication and Intimacy

When you begin to act in a way that impacts others close to you, you may begin to confront powerful psychological barriers, cultural and family taboos. You may come up against your worst fears as you push past a place of comfort.

People with AD/HD may have experienced confusion growing up because they were often blamed for things they didn't know how to change. Even though they were trying to please, they may have caused problems for others. They may have been told they spoke too loudly, made too many messes, interrupted, or in some way were just too much trouble for other important people in their lives. They may have felt left out or in the dark about what was going on.

As a result, situations encountered by adults that remind them in some way of those earlier situations, even though now they are diagnosed and see things more clearly, can often hit a nerve of vulnerability, triggering powerful feelings. You may on some level still fear a hurtful negative label will be hurled at you as retaliation for expressing your needs. To avoid this hurt, you may temporarily back away from some of the changes you were attempting to make.

So this is the watershed point. You have learned to value your differences and expanded your self-view. You know your dreams, your purpose, and what you need in order to operate well. But when it comes to translating all of this into the world with others, especially people close to you, you may hit powerful inhibitors.

It's important to know that this obstacle is to be expected; it's natural and can be worked through. If you know what is happening, it will be easier for you to step back a little and observe your feelings and triggers for a while until you are able to respond more thoughtfully instead of reacting with emotion.

It will help you at this point to observe and identify what is triggering your fears or old emotions. Let's say you find that when you want to ask for one of your needs to be met that affects another person in some way, you feel waves of anxiety come over you that you don't understand.

- **Just watch for a while. Remember when you felt like this before.**

- **What does it remind you of?**

- **What used to happen when you had special needs growing up?**

- **What were the reactions you got then?**

- **How did you know people were reacting negatively? Was it their words, the tone of their voice, a look on their face, or maybe a gesture?**

Although understanding does not eliminate fear, it does help reduce it and makes this process easier. So stick with the fear, observe it, notice when it materializes and why. Your task at this time is to observe and understand what you are reacting to so strongly. It might be another person's nonverbal message: tone of voice, gestures, or expression, such as a sigh, a raised eyebrow, or a dismissive wave of the hand. Or perhaps a certain phrase, one that challenges your motives or implies selfishness or laziness, takes you right back to an earlier time. For each of you, it will be different.

Now ask yourself the following questions:

- **Are you responding to an event or a relationship from your past? What is the worst-case scenario?**

- **What are you imagining would happen if you pushed through this taboo or upset the family balance?**

- **What messages do you have deeply embedded in you about getting these particular needs met?**

When you realize that these triggers have to do with a different time in your life, at an earlier point in your travels through AD/HD, they will start to lose some of their power over you. As time goes on, you will be able to take note of these triggers, feel the twinge of emotion, but still move forward. They won't stop you, or if they do, you will soon get back on track. Ascertaining the degree to which these triggers stop you is one way for you to gauge your own progress. Remember to go slowly.

Less-Than-Perfect Relationships

Especially when you're working to correct your self-view, at the beginning of the journey, you need to receive positive reflections, to be seen and accepted and to rid yourself of the relationships that are overwhelmingly toxic. As Dr. Edward Hallowell writes in his book *Connect,* it is important to "weed the garden" of bad relationships to make room for more healthy ones. He discusses the need to prune these relationships in order to continue to connect with people who are important to you.

As your view of your self is corrected, though, you become more able to hold on to it, even in the presence of people who are not perfectly accepting. This is important because the majority of our relationships are ones that we want or need, even though they are imperfect. Some people we are just plain stuck with, and we have to learn to accept their limitations when it comes to their understanding of our differences. Significant relationships include those with a spouse, partner, family, friends, teachers, bosses, or coworkers. At this point you will be able to tolerate these relationships more easily since you, not they, are defining your sense of self.

You don't have to refuse to share yourself at all with those who you feel don't understand you fully. Perfect understanding may never happen, and you might spend your whole life waiting for it. Just as in Journey Two you didn't wait to get over your AD/HD to begin to live, at this point you shouldn't wait for perfect understanding in order to come out and have full-close relationships. True understanding is a long-term process. But, as you know by now, it's a big enough job for you to understand yourself. I've learned that when you start to shift the way you feel about yourself, other people will make the shift along with you. As you come to understand yourself more fully and share this understanding with others, they will learn from you and your relationship will improve.

If adults wait for perfect understanding, they may direct their anger toward people who care about them and want to understand them, but who might never be completely able to do so. Adults with AD/HD may see this failure as a terrible lack of empathy. But to a certain degree it is unavoidable. It's like trying to understand the world of a blind person by closing your eyes. There is, of course, much more to living with blindness than this small experiment can ever reveal.

As you grow in your own acceptance of your differences, you will be able to tolerate other people's imperfect understanding more. They won't be able to affect you as much, and you will be able to affect them more: They begin to take their cues from you on what is acceptable behavior. I'm not saying that you should accept or tolerate abusive, disrespectful treatment from others because of your differences. These are toxic relationships and should be avoided. But, again, when you have an emotional investment with a person who can't quite "get it," you may want to consider keeping the parts of the relationship alive that are satisfying or important.

Protecting Yourself Mentally

If you have difficulty achieving this delicate balance with a person or in a situation that is apt to cause you problems, one approach is to find a way to protect yourself mentally even if, in reality, you are deliberately going to give up some of what you need in order to protect yourself. This conscious control and self-talk will make you feel less trapped and out of control and resentful. For instance, there are times when you will weigh your options and make the decision that, because of other values or needs, you will forgo your protection in order to connect. You might, for example, have a lot of work to do for a project but decide that you will go visit your grandmother who is lonely and who has called you up to invite you for a visit. You make this decision because visiting your grandmother is important to you, even though you know it will mean you will stay up very late that night to work and be tired the next day. This is different from automatically overcommitting, not choosing consciously, not knowing why, and just feeling overwhelmed and out of control. It's about choice, and it's about connecting when you want to, when you need to, when you choose to, not out of shame or guilt, embarrassment, or not knowing what to do.

When you are mentally in control and making such choices, you are aware of the reasons for your behavior. Anticipating the consequences makes it more likely that you'll be able to compensate for any problems you foresee. In the above example, you might cancel something less important scheduled for the next day, knowing you will need to catch up on sleep. These choices are short-term decisions, not an everyday lifestyle. It's analogous to choosing to go out in a thunderstorm to care for a sick friend, even though you are risking more than you would if you stayed home.

Connecting Verbally

When you can't fulfill your desire or another person's desire to actually connect, another alternative is to let that person know how much you want to connect with him at a specific time or in a certain situation even though you are unable to do so right now. When you decide you cannot give up the time or focus you need, the goal is to talk things over and make a plan to connect at some future time, and then follow through on this.

Whichever strategy you choose at the time, it is crucial somehow to convey to the other person how important he or she is to you. In addition to the obvious benefits of this, choosing one of these approaches defuses anxiety or avoidance, either of which might seriously damage the relationship. Sometimes it's best to connect instead of protect.

Many of these situations may not seem like a big deal to people who don't have AD/HD. For instance, most people are able to act in accordance with how much they care about other people, but for people with attention problems it is much more complex to always act out of a sense of their own values; they have to be taught to look at these issues this way. Their lack of follow-through on maintaining relationships is often misunderstood as a lack of caring. This is one of the painful parts of having AD/HD.

As one woman told me, "People are often unable to see my heart."

Giving Your Authentic Self (Without Losing Your Self)

The theme of this book is to value your differences. You've followed the stages of going from hiding them to valuing them to developing them to protecting them.

Now we confront the ultimate challenge and the most important—the true purpose of difference is to help you connect to others in an intimate way. You do this by giving who you are to others; giving your uniqueness, your thoughts, feelings, skills. This brings you and another person closer to each other by truly being known and opening yourself up to know someone else. There's no presenting a false front, no hiding your differences or apologizing for who you are; no running away from people who you feel are not like you. Such barriers would keep you from connecting, and you would miss the chance to enjoy and exchange differences that enrich you both.

When I talk about giving who you are to others, I'm referring to your authentic, true self. What often gets people into trouble in relationships is trying to give of themselves when their sense of self is not developed enough to set the limits and boundaries that protect them and make relationships comfortable and safe. Giving out of guilt or shame is counterproductive. What you wind up with is resentment or martyrdom or feeling of being depleted, without anything of real value to give to another person.

Karen Horney, a well-known psychoanalyst quoted earlier, defined the real self as the "alive, unique, personal center of ourselves that wants to grow." She also said, "When the real self is prevented from free healthy growth because of abandoning its needs to others, one can become alienated from it."[*] Keeping your real self alive and protecting it are vital, enabling you to give of yourself without becoming depleted and resentful in a relationship.

Beth's Difficult Relationships with Men

Like other single people with AD/HD, Beth confronted several issues as she entered into close relationships with men. Her level of social ease evolved as she made progress in dealing with her AD/HD.

In her late teens and early twenties, Beth noticed that, as hard as she tried, she could not keep a boyfriend for longer than a few months. She thought that she knew why. As everyone—mostly her family members—who had ever known her closely had said, she was messy. Even after diagnosis, she carefully hid anything about herself that might reveal or even hint at her messiness, determined to make a man like her.

Keeping this "big secret" about herself meant that she would never willingly invite anyone—not even a boyfriend she had been seeing for three months—to her apartment. When pushed to have someone over, she would run herself ragged rushing home after work to cram things into closets and drawers. She also made it a policy never to do anything without days of advance notice, so that she could make sure her hair was right and nothing about her outfit would betray her messiness to her date. When she was late or disorganized in any way, she would quickly come up with a lie

---

[*]Quote is attributed to Karen Horney in *The Adopted Self* by Betty Jean Lifton (New York: Basic Books, 1994).

Sparks Fly from Differences

Differences aren't the enemies of relationships. It's hiding your differences and uniqueness that keeps you apart, keeps you from being fully known. Having a separate self is a vital ingredient that makes intimacy possible in a healthy and interesting relationship. Adults with AD/HD often grow up sensitive to being different, though, and so have a difficult time feeling comfortable with this.

The sparks that fly from differences can cause excitement, making relationships vital and alive. And when someone else really knows you—differences and all—that's the true definition of intimacy.

to conceal this fact. Often, instead of calling to tell a date that she was going to be late for coffee or dinner, she would call and claim that she was ill. When she was caught in these lies, she was unwilling to reveal herself and would give no explanation for her behavior. Naturally, men who tried to get close to Beth had a difficult time understanding her.

Beth found it exhausting to keep this secret. At some point either she had to end the relationship because she couldn't keep up the deception, or her boyfriend would break up with her because he couldn't get beyond her standoffishness.

Whenever another boyfriend would move on, she believed it was because he had found out her secret. She held on to this belief despite the fact that past boyfriends had told her outright that they felt there was something distant and unknowable about her that made it difficult to get close to her.

Beth needed to see that she, not her AD/HD, was chasing people away.

Over time, as she changed the way she felt about her AD/HD, she was able to be open about other aspects of her self, such as her warmth, humor, compassion, and talent.

Jennifer in Journey Three

When Jennifer noticed that it was much easier for her to prepare meals without the distraction of the stereo playing in the neighboring family room, she realized she needed to reduce this stimulus. In Journey One, Jennifer had not known this about herself; but even if she had, she would not have felt entitled to make such a request, because she then felt that her AD/HD had already created so many problems in her family and she did not want to risk causing any more upsets. But by Journey Three, she felt entitled to ask for this need to be met. However, she found that whenever the stereo came on, she could not get her husband to turn it off.

Her few attempts at politely asking to have the stereo moved to a different area or to please turn it down were ignored or dismissed as silly. She began to nag or grumble, and a couple of times she went into a full rage and stormed out—anything to try to get her needs acknowledged. Her husband continued to ignore her.

After a while, she found that she was afraid to make this request again, that she would get an awful knot in her stomach and waves of fear at the thought of asking him to make such a big change in his routine and comfort to accommodate her needs. Jennifer had come up against a psychological barrier to expressing her needs and having them met.

For a long time, Jennifer felt this fear without understanding it. As a result, she was unwilling to act, since a large, unknown wall of fear stood in her way. This period of seeming inaction lasted for months. While you may think that inaction is a poor or passive response, in fact there was a great deal of activity going on under the surface as Jennifer observed and made sense of her responses. Taking your time in situations like this can be a constructive response if you sense the opportunity for observation, reflection, and understanding.

I encourage adults who begin the difficult process of letting themselves be known to take their time with this fear—especially when dealing with family members and those closest to them. When you feel that you understand your fear better, you can begin to act. But allow yourself plenty of time before taking action. Jennifer's pause at this point was both natural and beneficial. It allowed her to notice her fear and understand it.

Jennifer came to realize that she feared she wasn't important enough for anyone to make changes and was afraid that this message would surface if she pushed for her needs to be met. She was sensitive and vulnerable to any hint that she was stupid or insignificant because of her history. Even though she had had friends growing up, she often felt she was not taken seriously, was written off as dumb or spacey. People might have enjoyed her company, but she was not included or respected when a serious discussion came up. She had never felt she was seen for her real abilities. This was the painful hook she wanted to avoid. Once she understood that she was being hooked and stopped by her husband's dismissive attitude, she was able to break some of its power—aided by medication, support (including therapy and her AD/HD group), and her changing perception of herself.

Eventually, through this process, Jennifer could see that having her requests met was absolutely essential to her well-being. She was no longer willing to be cognitively incapacitated by a blasting stereo. And she was no longer willing to be ignored, because she had learned to take herself and her needs seriously enough. After making these internal changes, she was ready to put her inner resolve into words and had a better chance of getting the results she wanted. For you can communicate more successfully when you fully feel committed to your needs and are clear about what Harriet Lerner, in *The Dance of Anger*, calls your "bottom lines."

At this point Jennifer was able to come up with a variety of solutions or approaches that took her needs as well as her husband's into consideration. She didn't wait for him to agree or for him to take the lead; she didn't say, "Please let's do something about this," which had left her feeling she had no control in the past.

At a quiet and calm time, Jennifer offered her husband a few options. There were times when the stereo was not a problem—when she wasn't preparing dinner or when she was out for the evening and wouldn't be affected by the music. She suggested that she might also enjoy the music with him, and on those nights they could order in a pizza or bring in dinner, eliminating the need for her to prepare food. Another option was to put a speaker in a room downstairs and listen to the music there. There were many other options that could be considered, but she made it clear that this was a critical issue and she didn't back down. (She had not been able to do this earlier, when she was more vulnerable to anticipated attacks.) She was then able to communicate in some way, verbally or nonverbally, "It is absolutely necessary we have this conversation." Even if she didn't use these exact words, the following message was transmitted: "These are the alternatives. I'm not willing to live like this anymore. [But you must mean it!] Let's find a calm time to discuss this further. I take myself seriously. I take your concerns seriously, as well. I know it's inconvenient for you. These are alternatives I can see that could work for both of us. What are your ideas? I need to have this issue worked out before a specific date."

Jennifer ran the risk of provoking her husband's anger or even an implied threat of abandonment, such as "I'll just go out to a bar where I can get some peace!" These are "change-back" messages and can be very frightening and difficult to withstand. Had she encountered them, she might have needed more support.

After a while Jennifer reported that her husband suddenly stopped fighting her. She told me: "He came home the other day and said, 'I had a great idea! I bought this set of headphones for the stereo! I'll wear them when you are making dinner!'" His decision to buy the headphones wasn't really a coincidence. It is important for Jennifer to realize it was the result of staying with her needs, pushing through these barriers, and waiting it out while her husband regained his balance—and while both of them moved to a new and better way of relating.

For adults with AD/HD who have begun to connect with others and ask that their needs be met, the fear that others will dismiss them for being weird, messy, stupid, lazy, and so on, may still get in their way.

Don in Journey Three

When Don was growing up, he often had a hard time focusing in social situations, which meant he often said very little or entered into conversations with awkward and inappropriate comments. As a result, he was often left out, laughed at, or picked on by his peers. It's not surprising that he developed a great fear of rejection. When Don became an adult, he dealt with this fear by hiding his true, creative self beneath the conservative façade of an insurance salesman who wore the same clothes and had the same haircut as his peers. He was also careful not to let himself say too much around others, lest he once again come out with something weird or off the wall. When Don began to shed this façade as he developed his self-concept, this fear of rejection resurfaced.

After Don began developing his self-concept, his way of dealing with the people he supervised at his insurance company started to change. He became a more direct supervisor, communicating to his employees exactly what he expected of them. One employee in particular responded by giving him a "change-back" message that triggered his fear of rejection. This employee would often mention to Don what fun he and other guys had had together over the weekend or during the last sales trip. He teased him with remarks like "It's too bad you have to spend a lot of your extra time organizing those nasty files." This employee, part of the "in" group at work, took Don right back to the teasing he had faced in grade school. Try as he might, Don couldn't assert himself when he needed to give any kind of corrective feedback to this man. Don didn't want to rock the boat or put himself in a position where this man might communicate in some way, "You're too weird to be with us."

At this point, Don "changed back" temporarily rather than confront his fear of rejection and state his position more firmly with his problem employee.

But eventually he came to understand that whereas in his childhood he'd had little power or control in these kinds of situations, he was now in a position of authority. When he recognized this difference, he was able to claim that power and act in his best interest, changing the skewed power dynamics.

Like Don, you may change back for a time, then advance again later and reassert yourself. Retreating to an old way of behaving is often temporary and is a natural part of Journey Three. So don't feel defeated if you find yourself hesitating and making an about-face when your fears rise up. This is all part of your growth process.

In the next chapter we will look at more strategies for making connections with others. Bear in mind that implementing these strategies doesn't automatically guarantee that you will have healthy relationships. To have healthy relationships, you must construct a healthy self-view, and this takes time. Connecting with others involves a deep shift in the way you understand and value yourself.

Explorations

Where Do You Stand on the Protection/Connection Continuum?

- Do you tend to spend your time at one end or the other, at some point along this continuum, or in the center zone where you are able to maintain both healthy connection and healthy self-protection?

- What happens when you go too far in one direction?

- Can you remember a situation in which you were overprotecting or overconnecting?

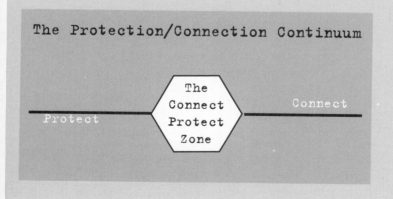

The Protection/Connection Continuum

The Connect Protect Zone

Protect   Connect

- Think about a situation in which you had a choice between connecting with others and protecting your self. Which choice did you make? How did you make it? Was your choice deliberate, or was it involuntary, leaving you with resentment?

- Think about a situation in which you wanted to connect but chose to protect your needs. Why did you make this choice? What did you say to the other person or people?

- Think about a current relationship that is important to you but which causes you to tip to one side or the other of the protection/connection continuum. What would you need to achieve a better balance in this relationship?

What Would Happen If . . . ?

- What sacred traditions in your family need to be confronted if you are to operate well?

- What family dynamic or fear might be holding you back?

- What would be the worst thing that you can imagine happening if you went ahead with expressing your need?

- In what way does this situation remind you of your childhood experiences?

- **How are you different now? How are you better equipped to deal with the outcome?**

Test new responses slowly. Don't try and change everything at once. Notice the rules operating in your family. Notice the patterns of interaction. Notice what's going on between people when your feelings are triggered. Think about actually putting into place those changes that you desire and how this will involve other people's feelings.

Circle the following barriers that apply to you?

- **Fear of conflict**
- **Fear of change**
- **Fear of rejection**
- **Upsetting and rebalancing power in the family**
- **Setting limits, saying no to others' needs**
- **Challenging sacred family and cultural traditions**
- **Questioning longstanding roles, as well as spoken and unspoken rules**
- **Saying yes to myself feels selfish**

Ask yourself and begin to notice

- **What triggers you?**
- **What hooks you?**
- **What stops you?**

10

Communicating
for Connection

Y OU MAY HAVE CONQUERED the way you feel about yourself, know what you need, and have moved passed the internal barriers, but you're still stumped when it comes to communicating in difficult situations. This chapter contains a model to use when describing your differences or setting limits in your relationships.

Beginning to be more open about your struggles provides an opportunity to explore the other person's feelings and helps you determine how he or she feels about your differences—important information to take into account when determining if the relationship should go any farther. By discussing these difficulties and differences, not only do you get to know the other person, but the other person gets to know you. Openness about your difference helps deepen the discussion on many issues. It has to come at the right time, though, and with the right people, so go slowly as you test the waters.

It can be especially difficult to talk about your differences when you are just beginning to date or become involved in an intimate relationship that may not feel safe yet. Nevertheless, discussing matters that you might not have to at this point, discussing these issues early on, gives you a window into this potential partner. It gives you information about the person that is critical long before there are discussions about long-term commitments, such as living together or marriage. It's one way to protect yourself from choosing the wrong partner. On the flip side, one of the best things a person with AD/HD can do, according to Dr. Edward Hallowell, is marry the right person.

Beth Faces a Communication Challenge

One night while Beth and her friends were out dancing at a nightclub, she met a young man named Jerry. Before long, the two started dating. But this time, because of the progress she had made, she was able to approach the beginning stages of the relationship in a new way. She was now more willing to say what she was thinking or feeling. When difficult situations would arise, she could describe or talk about her differences in a way that simply described the facts rather than characterized her in a negative way. Unlike her other relationships, this one was not based on secrecy. (At this point in a relationship, you don't necessarily have to talk about the AD/HD diagnosis. Just describe your difficulties, and remember to talk as much about your strengths as your challenges!)

The first time that Beth had invited Jerry to her apartment, she made arrangements to leave her volunteer job early so she would have plenty of time to straighten up before nine o'clock, when he was due to arrive to watch a video. But on the day of their date, Jerry called Beth and asked her to meet him right after work at a new restaurant nearby. He suggested after dinner that they could go back to her place and watch a video, as they had originally planned. This created a problem for Beth. On the one hand (the connection side of the equation), she loved the idea and appreciated the invitation. But on the other hand (the protection side), this new plan would make it virtually impossible for her to tidy up her apartment. She did not want to pretend anymore, and she did not want to run herself ragged. She also knew that she wasn't ready to have Jerry see her apartment in its "natural" state. She wanted to be open with him so he could begin to know her, but it seemed premature to tell him the extent of her differences.

The communication challenge she faced was to express the connect and the protect side and then make some suggestions that incorporated both sides to her satisfaction. She might, for example, say to him: "Jerry, what a great idea. I really appreciate the invitation. I've been wanting to try that new restaurant, and it certainly would make sense to meet there after work. [Connect.] The only problem I have is that I was expecting to have several hours after work to get the apartment and myself straightened up so I could really enjoy the video and our time together. I'm working on a special project [here she emphasizes her strengths] and I tend to be disorganized at home while I'm preoccupied with work. I know it probably doesn't matter to you if the place is somewhat messy, but it's important to me to have it be special tonight." Or: "I have a difficult time with organizing and still feel self-conscious about having you over when the place is a mess. I wanted the place to be special for tonight."

Next she might offer a couple of suggestions: "We could

postpone the dinner out for another night, go ahead with the original plan, and bring in some food and eat while we watch the video. Or we could meet at the restaurant and save the video for another night or go to a movie after dinner. Which plan sounds better to you? Either one is fine with me."

Jerry would probably respond by trying to reassure Beth that it wasn't important to him what her place looked like. But at this point, she wasn't ready to take the chance of showing him her messy apartment. She was, however, clear about the choices that worked for her and might have felt confident enough to say lightly, "I know it's weird, but it's just one of my idiosyncrasies." Or, if she was ready to open up more: "We could talk about this over dinner, if you like."

The above scenario demonstrates how to communicate effectively when confronted with a difficult situation. Beth didn't overwhelm Jerry with too much information right away; nor did she retreat or return to her earlier ways of coping that had left her feeling depleted. She acknowledged how much she appreciated his offer and communicated that she would love to go to the new restaurant. She also started the process of allowing each of them to explore their unique ways of being, which would bring them closer to finding out if they were compatible and if they enjoyed being open with each other about their vulnerabilities and struggles.

The work at this stage very much revolves around these kinds of communication issues. By this point, even though you may have come to value yourself, you may still not know how to communicate in a way that demonstrates this to others.

MUTUALLY RESPECTFUL RELATIONSHIPS

All mutually respectful relationships can be characterized as follows: Each party validates the other's feelings, point of view, or wishes, at the same time setting limits and communicating his or her own needs and differences. This allows you to get your needs met and to remain in contact with the other person without feeling depleted (as you would if you sacrificed the protect side of the equation). So in the end you are able to give more, not less.

Not Practicing What I Preach

Many people don't communicate their needs or don't validate others' feelings because they feel too vulnerable—or they try to protect themselves by not communicating at all. Sometimes in an effort not to appear rude or weird, we wind up doing just that.

On one occasion, a few minutes before I gave a workshop on this subject to a large crowd, a woman approached and started talking to me. In those few minutes before I start to speak, my mind is occupied on what seems like a million details as I try to make sure I know what I want to say and that all the equipment is working properly. Usually, if anyone asks me something or talks to me at this point, I tell him to see me after the presentation. But this time, not wanting to appear rude, I had pretended to give her my full attention even though I couldn't. Not only were we not connecting; I also was unable to do what I knew I had to do to protect myself.

At some point I realized how ironic it was to be giving a presentation on this topic within minutes of mishandling the very same situation. I addressed the issue at that presentation and explored what I could have done differently that would have both protected myself and kept the connection. I could have said something like "I want to give you my full attention, but I find I'm unable to do that right before giving a speech. So please, let's talk afterward."

That sounds very simple, but it can be difficult to remember when you're overwhelmed at the time with conflicting desires. As we've seen, it's very challenging to maintain a balance between protecting and connecting, and it requires constant vigilance on your part.

Five Steps to Safe and Assertive AD/HD Communication

This section offers a simple five-step model that you can think about when you're in a difficult situation, one that challenges you to communicate your differences and difficulties.

Many relationships go by the wayside because in the initial stages the person with AD/HD feels ashamed and embarrassed and withdraws. It doesn't have to be this way. You can learn to validate the other person's uniqueness and needs, while maintaining your own self-worth and boundaries. This model focuses on the special concerns and needs of an adult with AD/HD and applies to a variety of situations and relationships. When you're confronted with a challenging AD/HD interpersonal situation, try these five steps. The goal is to validate the other person's feelings or needs, to communicate that you want to connect, and to describe what you need. The trick is not to put yourself down as you do this. Remember, words will sometimes fail you; when that happens, regroup and try again. This is to be expected. The process is ongoing.

I've dubbed this model the SAFETY model to give you an easy way to remember the steps:

1. **S eparate AD/HD from your core sense of self.**

2. **F igure out what you need.**

3. **E xpress your understanding and appreciation of the other person.**

4. **T ell the other person about your difficulty and your need.**

5. **Y ou give suggestions.**

The first two steps are internal. You take them before you *say anything* to the other person!

STEP 1. SEPARATE AD/HD FROM YOUR CORE SENSE OF SELF

Ask yourself:

- **What faulty thinking am I using?**

- **What kind of self-talk ties your AD/HD to your value as a person?**

Try to form a statement in your mind that describes what you are saying to yourself that ties your difficulties to your sense of self or the power dynamics in your relationships. This is the hook that causes problems for you in negotiations with others. When confronted with a problematic communication situation, take a moment to examine your self-talk by mentally filling in these blanks: *Because* I have difficulty with _____, I think I _____.

The following are examples of negative self-talk:

- **Because I have difficulty with organizing my papers, I think I'm stupid.**

- **Because I have trouble balancing my checkbook, I have to give up all control of my finances to someone else.**

- **Because I have difficulty being on time, I think my partner has the right to put me down, saying that I'm irresponsible or immature.**

Remember, what you are doing here is trying to identify this pairing so you can separate your AD/HD from your core value.

Next ask yourself: What can I say to myself that helps me separate my AD/HD from the core sense of myself (instead of connecting it as in the preceeding statements)? You do this by taking the statement and slightly rephrasing it to yourself. "*Even though* I have difficulty with _____, that doesn't mean _____." For example, "Even though I have difficulties organizing my papers, that doesn't mean I'm stupid." Substituting *even though* for *because* is a simple change that leads to a critical difference in meaning!

Here are a few examples of other forms these statements can take:

- **Even though _____, it's not OK for you to _____.**

- **Even though _____, I still have the right to _____.**

- **Even though _____, I still have the ability to _____.**

- **Even though _____, I still have enough value to _____.**

A similar example of corrective self-talk:

- **I am _____, but that has nothing to do with _____.**

When addressing your difficulties with organization, you might say, "I am disorganized, but that has nothing to do with my value as a person."

STEP 2. FIGURE OUT WHAT YOU NEED

This step also takes place internally as self-talk. Ask yourself:

- **What do I need to do to make this situation work for me?**

- **What is it I really need or want in order to keep functioning well?**

- **Is there something I need to do, something I need to ask someone else to do?**

Think back to what you learned about how you operate successfully, or consider what conditions are present when things go well in your life now.

Next, list the help or support you may need. You may need concrete help, as in the following examples:

- **I need help with organizing my personal finances or paying bills.**

- **I need to have directions written down for me at work.**

You may also need emotional help:

- **I need emotional support or to be treated with respect.**

- **I need to avoid or deflect toxic help.**

- **I need to not be yelled at.**

Now list what conditions need to be present for you to make a situation work for you. (Remember, these needs might affect others, so it would be more difficult for you to put solutions into place!) For example:

- **I need reduced stimulation.**

- **I need more structure.**

- **I need a breather from an overwhelming situation for a while.**

Finally, list what you may need to do for yourself. You may need to set limits. For example: "When someone asks me to do something I have difficulty with, I'll offer to substitute a task for which I'm suited better." Or you may need to make a choice. For example, "I need Sue's help to get organized, but I won't ask her because she belittles me." Bear in mind that others can't understand or give you what you need if you don't know how you operate and aren't willing to let them know. To know what you will need, you may need to review chapter 8 to determine what variables are in place when things are working well for you. Remember, focus on problem solving, not you as the problem!

In steps 1 and 2 you've done the inner preparation that will allow you now in steps 3–5 to form a few simple sentences to say aloud to others. These next statements will validate the other person, describe your difficulties and needs, and offer alternative solutions based on your strengths as well as the needs of the other person.

Validating the other person's feelings or understanding his point of view and needs or the effect your AD/HD has had on him is important in this process. Step 3 is the one that can keep your connection alive: making a simple statement about working toward a solution that is mutually agreeable. This is different from excessive apologizing that irritates other people after a while and keeps you feeling stuck in a "bad" position. It's not about placating him or simply blowing him off with an apology. Your statement can show the other person that you recognize and validate something of importance to him, or that you recognize his frustration and care about it, and could be as simple as "I understand you are frustrated' or "I see this is very important to you." But it's an important component of the communication process.

Earlier, you most likely would have felt that if you tried this, you would open up a can of worms, bring on a torrent of criticism. Even now, step 3 might still be a very difficult step to take. It is this acknowledging of the other person's position, though, that often makes the vital difference between whether you connect or disconnect.

STEP 4. TELL THE OTHER PERSON
ABOUT YOUR DIFFICULTY AND YOUR NEED

Once you know what you need and have eliminated many of the hooks we discussed in the previous chapter, it will be easier for you to take this step. Begin by memorizing the phrase "describe, don't characterize." Now describe your difference or difficulty and/or need or limits instead of globalizing or characterizing. This applies to yourself as well as to the other person. Examples: "I have great difficulty with organizing my paperwork" (which describes your difficulty) instead of "I am lazy or stupid or a mess or immature" (which globalizes and characterizes yourself). "I have difficulty with organizing my paperwork, and I need you to stop putting me down" (which describes difficulty and expresses your need) instead of "I need you to stop being such a jerk like you always are" (globalizing and characterizing the other person).

STEP 5. YOU GIVE SUGGESTIONS

Taking a proactive stand may help you feel more control in a challenging situation rather than feeling that you need to give up all personal power and respect because you have difficulties or differences or needs. In this step you begin the process of negotiation by offering alternatives based on your needs and your strengths or what you're willing to do and with what modifications. At the same time, remember to acknowledge or validate the other person. So, in general, reframe situations to reflect your strengths.

Examples: "This is really important to me, so I want to take my time and think it through carefully"—instead of confessing in a self-deprecating tone, "I'm not quick-witted." Offer a suggestion by restructuring the task, or propose that something be done in a different way or form than originally requested. When asked to perform or contribute from an area of difficulty, you could reply, "I won't be able to _____, but I'd be happy to [fill in the blank with a strength]" or "I propose [offer of strengths]. How would that work?"

Handling Difficult Situations at Work

If your boss has given you a project to complete and you're having trouble accomplishing the task, don't wait until the deadline to communicate the problem. You could say, "I'm finding the project very interesting [step 3], but it's taking longer than I expected [step 4]. I could finish on time if I get some help, or I could continue working alone if the deadline can be extended [step 5]."

When someone is trying to talk with you in a distracting environment, try something like the following statement (you'll notice you never have to mention AD/HD! Just stick with the description of the difficulty and need): "I find that when it's noisy I have a difficult time concentrating on what you're saying [tell or describe], and I really want to hear what you're saying [express appreciation]."

When someone is explaining something to you that is important for you to remember, you might explain your note taking by saying, "I find I have a difficult time remembering the details you're telling me unless I write them down [tell or describe], and I don't want to keep interrupting your work to ask what comes next [express appreciation]."

Handling Difficult Situations Relating to Social Events

Instead of simply disappearing when you feel bombarded at a party or family gathering, you can describe what you are doing without actually validating out loud. Sometimes just mentioning what you are doing automatically validates more than just withdrawing without a word. You might say: "I tend to feel overloaded at these events. I need a little fresh air. Just wanted you to know I'll be back in fifteen minutes. I'm going to take a walk." Then people won't think you are weird, or at least you won't feel they think you are, which may cause you to withdraw more.

When you're asked to contribute in some way that is difficult for you, offer to substitute something that is a strength of yours. Here is an example of what I mean: "It's important to me to contribute to the holiday get-together [express appreciation], but baking is not something I do [tell or describe]. However, I do play the guitar and could sing some Christmas songs [your suggestions or alternatives]. How would that be?"

How to Deal with Toxic Help

Toxic help is when someone helping you with a task acts as if that help buys them the right to take over, criticize, dismiss you, treat you like a child, insult you, or do anything that generally feels bad to you. Often a person with AD/HD will put up with this because he feels that in some way he is bad or that his difficulties are shameful and on some level he deserves to be treated badly. You may be so desperate for the help that you swallow your feelings just to get whatever you need taken care of. But it's possible to accept help and set limits at the same time.

Suppose your non-AD/HD partner or parent is helping you write checks to pay your bills and says to you, while dealing with late notices and unorganized piles: "What is the matter with you? How can you live like this?" Or: "What kind of example are you setting for your children?"

This situation may trigger self-talk that is based on faulty thinking:

- "I'm a lousy person and a real burden. I'll just let her [or him] yell. At least we'll get the bills paid."

- "I am such a stupid and immature person [or bad partner]."

- "I better not say anything, because he [or she] is right."

Approach the situation using the five-step SAFETY model. Start with step 1: Separate AD/HD from your core sense of self. Examine your internal self-talk. Ask yourself: What faulty thinking am I using? "I'm thinking that I'm already too much trouble and deserve any anger that comes my way, because I really messed up."

Ask yourself: "What can I say to myself that helps me separate my AD/HD from the core sense of myself?" You may say: "I have difficulty in this area of organization, but it's not OK for anyone to treat me badly." Or: "I'm not a stupid, incompetent person. I have severe organizational problems, but actually I am pretty smart. I certainly don't deserve to be treated like this just to get my bills paid."

Next, use step 2: Figure out what you need. Ask yourself: "What is it I need to do to make this situation work for me?" Return to chapter 9 if you need help identifying the conditions under which you operate well. Your self-talk might include statements like:

- **I need to get bills paid.**

- **I need to have this person stop putting me down.**

- **I know this is going to set me back. I don't have to accept this just because I have problems.**

- **I need him [or her] to stop putting me down, and I need help with my bills— but not at this price. I may need to find a different way to get help for now.**

If you have trouble at this point, you may need to go back to work on your acceptance of your difficulties and the impact they are having on your self-view. You may need to think back to the strengths you've discovered and have come to value.

If you are able to figure out what you need, proceed to step 3: Express (out loud) your understanding and appreciation to the other person. Validate the other person's needs or feelings: "I know it's frustrating to work with me on the bills and find them in this condition." Or: "I know you are trying to help."

Then move to step 4: Tell the other person about your difficulty and your need. Remember to describe your difficulty (or difference) or your need (or limits.) Don't characterize yourself by saying, *"I know I'm an idiot"* or *"I'm impossible to work with."* You could say, *"Organizing and paying bills is a difficult task for me, and I can see it's frustrating to you. But it's not OK for you to talk like that, and it's not working. I need you to stop putting me down if we are going to continue to work together."*

Close by following step 5: You give suggestions. Offer alternatives based on your needs and your strengths. Start the process of negotiation.

"I need you to not keep criticizing me while you are helping, since it just makes me feel worse or angry and I'm not willing to pay that price. These are the options I can come up with.

"I can contribute more so you don't feel you are doing it all alone. I could write down the bills we are paying, or trade with you to do something you have a hard time with so you won't feel resentful.

"I'd be happy to work with you on devising a new system of keeping track of the due dates and keeping the bills organized. Actually, I'm good at thinking of systems. It's just the maintenance that's difficult for me. Maybe we can go through the bills together and I'll write the day they are due on the calendar; then we can meet each week and follow up on this together. Would that work for you?

"If you can't help me without putting me down, I can get someone else to help me until we are able to work together. Or we can take a little break when you get frustrated."

How Would You Handle This Situation?

You have been asked to volunteer for a good cause at work, but you are not good at the task you've been asked to perform. In addition, the situation itself is a pro-blem for you, and you don't have the time. The challenge is to set limits without cutting yourself off from your co-workers.

A colleague says: "This is such a good cause. A bunch of us are going to sit down and have a mailing party on Saturday. All we have to do is copy, collate, stamp, address, and stuff envelopes while we chat. It'll be fun and won't take that much time."

What will you say to yourself? Perhaps: "This would be a nightmare for me. They wouldn't believe that I, a successful executive, would have a hard time trying to copy, collate, and talk simultaneously. I would be an absolute mess. What is wrong with me? A second-grader could do this. I am already overwhelmed as it is; giving up a Saturday right now would put me over the top. But they'll think I'm selfish or unfriendly if I say no. I'll go—I'll just have to stay up all night to get everything else done."

Using step 1: You will separate AD/HD from your core self, and revise your self-talk: "Pretending will move me away from people. Depleting myself more isn't the answer. I know it's easy for other people to do these things, but it's really a problem for me and I'm not willing to create such anxiety for myself. I'm not dumb or selfish or immature just because I'm not a great collator."

Guided by step 2 (you will figure out what you need), continue your self-talk: "I need to find a way to offer what I can contribute that would actually feel good to me, like entertaining at the annual fund-raiser, which other people can't do as well, or I need to find a way to keep healthy and focused on what I'm already involved in while not pushing them away."

Next, using step 3, you will acknowledge and validate your colleague's position by saying to her: "I see this is a very important cause to you and I wish I could help you in that way."

There's no reason to add, "I'm completely useless at these kinds of tasks," unless you can actually say that and believe it with humor. Nor should you say, "I'm overwhelmed and overloaded and depressed and have AD/HD." Those are not the ways to talk about your difficulty—step 4.

Instead, follow up by saying: "I find I'm unable to add anything else to my plate right now."

Finally, using step 5, you will offer some suggestions: "Please call me next time, or let me take some flyers and I'll put them up as I do errands. I can write a check or help out in some other way, such as entertaining at the fund-raiser [which is your strength]." Or: "I find I'm unable to spare the time now. I know this is important and I would like to contribute in some way."

Remember, the point of all this communication is to connect with others, maintain your self-respect, and protect your special needs so you can keep operating well. You may have improved your self-view a great deal, in which case this will be easier, but communicating this view and getting your needs expressed is still a whole new skill. In the "Explorations" section of this chapter you will have a chance to practice these ways of communication; keep practicing until they become more natural.

In the next chapter we will look at how Jennifer, Don, Beth, and Lance learned to communicate for connection and protection.

Explorations

Make up your own scenarios from real situations in your own life; then, following the SAFETY model, come up with suggestions for responding. Practice alone, with a partner, or in a group. The main point is to keep using this model so it becomes natural. You may want to keep the model with you—(see appendix A)—in your pocket or purse or wallet and refer to it when you're faced with an emergency.

First, think of a difficult situation that you are anticipating or one that you have experienced. Next, describe the scenario. What does the other person say to you? Then ask yourself these questions:

1. **What is your self-talk? Are you using any faulty thinking? Turn it into a statement that separates AD/HD from your core sense of self.**

2. **Ask yourself what is it you need to make the situation work for you.**

3. **What might you say (aloud) to validate the other person's point of view or feelings?**

4. **What would you say that describes your need and difficulty or your difference without characterizing or globalizing yourself or the other person?**

5. **What might you suggest based on your strengths and your needs?**

Write a paragraph to put these components together.

Journey's End: Measuring Success from the Inside

WHEN I WAS A LITTLE GIRL, my family and I took a long cross-country trip by car. As soon as we got started, I began asking my parents if *we were there yet*. And I kept asking them every few hours. I missed the beautiful mountains and lakes and the color of magnificent sunsets that my mother kept trying to get me to look at and appreciate. All I could think about was getting "there," even though I really had no idea what was so great about where we were going. I obviously missed the point that the experiences along the way were an important part of the trip.

I often see that same impatience and misperception regarding the length, scope, and complexity of the AD/HD voyage. Adults often place mistaken emphasis on the final destination, rather than noticing the growth they're experiencing at each step along the way.

At the end of your trip what you will find is just more of *you*—not an artificial goal, not the complete elimination of your AD/HD symptoms, and not a different or fixed person. Speed is not important or even possible when you start out on this trip. There is no perfect end point. What is important is to just start out and keep making midcourse corrections that keep you headed in the right direction. Even a slight adjustment of angle, of view, will take you in a whole new direction.

The struggle is part of life with AD/HD. This is a difficult thing to accept, but acceptance will ultimately free up a lot of energy to refocus on your life. Rabbi Larry Kushner makes a similar point in *The Book of Words: Talking Spiritual Life; Living Spiritual Talk*. He notes that we sometimes wonder why we are having such a difficult time and ask, "Why are there so many obstacles in our path?" Then he provides the answer: "The obstacles do not block our way. They are our way."*

AD/HD is one of the great challenges in your life—but it is *not* your life. It is a description of the way your brain operates, not a description of you as a person. If you can accept this, you can relax somewhat and work with it, instead of fighting so hard against it.

Measuring Success from the Inside

You can't judge whether the treatment of the adult with AD/HD has been successful exclusively on the basis of outer—that is, observable—changes. In some cases, outer symptoms might not look that much better, but real improvements have been made nonetheless. Success is about how you feel about yourself, your ability to lead your life, to have a new sense of vitality, and to have satisfying relationships. The shifts start deep inside, and as you progress, significant changes can be occurring beneath the surface before anyone else can see anything happening. It is important for

* Rabbi Larry Kushner, *The Book of Words: Talking Spiritual Life; Living Spiritual Talk* (Woodstock, VT: Jewish Lights Publishing, 1993), pp. 99–101.

you and the people trying to help you to know this in order to monitor and guide your progress. Such shifts are the building blocks for a long-term successful and satisfying voyage through the rest of adulthood.

LOCKED IN MY MESSY CLOSET

To illustrate how important it is not to judge yourself or anyone else exclusively by what is observable, but to also consider the inner view of self, I offer the following personal story.

A few years ago, after the publication of my book *Women with Attention Deficit Disorder*, I was often invited to speak to different groups. I was especially pleased at one point when I was invited to deliver a keynote address on the subject of women with AD/HD to a statewide mental health conference. A few days from the conference, I was in my office working on this speech, when I got a phone call from the chairperson to work out the details of my arrival. I hung up the phone feeling pretty good, then decided to take a break. I walked through (or waded through) two-foot-high stacks of papers and reached for the doorknob. I felt nothing. I looked down, and then I remembered the doorknob had fallen off sometime during that extremely busy week. It was probably somewhere in the room, but I had no idea where. By now the papers weren't really piles anymore; they were just a vast sea threatening to overtake me. Anyone using this moment to assess my progress would have been sure that I had not made any progress! But what I said and did next, I believe, are more significant markers. I didn't say: "Forget it! What a stupid jerk. How am I supposed to talk to these people? What do I have to say? I can't even open my door. I will have to wait until I don't lose doorknobs or make so many messes before I allow myself to move on. I'll call the whole thing off."

Instead, I laughed at the absurdity of my situation: For so long, I had been speaking to others about coming out of the messy closet and here I was actually locked in my messy office. Then I did something I might not have done earlier on in my AD/HD travels: called for help. I telephoned friends, who came over with a screwdriver and a ladder. Years ago, I might have just sat there all day waiting for my husband to come several hours later, because I would have been too embarrassed to let anyone else know what had happened. The point is: Don't assess the success of treatment or determine someone's progress solely by observable primary symptoms. Take into consideration the person's self-view and how his actions follow from that more authentic view of self.

Jennifer Takes a Stand

In Journey One, even after diagnosis and treatment, Jennifer's entire life revolved around her AD/HD and her deficits. She had to work through the way she viewed her symptoms before she could allow herself to get the support she needed. Jennifer still placed herself in a one-down position with her husband, because her difficulties made her feel guilty for anything bad that happened. She felt that, because of the problems her AD/HD had caused, she did not deserve to ask for her needs to be fulfilled. Along with this, she felt that when her AD/HD struck, her husband could treat her in toxic and even at times emotionally abusive ways.

Like so many partners and spouses of adults with AD/HD, Jennifer's husband sometimes understandably felt upset with her behavior since it impacted their life together. He even felt that her lateness or forgetfulness was a personal attack on him, a gesture of thoughtlessness or indifference. When Jennifer would show up late, he'd feel hurt, lose his temper, and lash out with cruel comments. "You're as bad as a child. You really are," he'd say. Or: "How can you call yourself a responsible adult if you can't even make it to a lunch date on time? Are you just lazy? Are you stupid? Is that what your problem is?"

Convinced on some level that she deserved these attacks, Jennifer endured them even though her occasional lateness and blunders were not meant to hurt her husband. They were just a part of her AD/HD. But because she was stuck in self-distortion, she could not really distinguish between herself and her AD/HD. Her first steps were to expand her view of herself and gain some perspective on this situation; then she realized that her difficulties needed to be addressed for what they were—just problems with lateness and organization. Next, she strategized in order to compensate for her difficulties. At the same time, though, she needed to limit the way in which her husband could express his frustration with her. Her diagnosis, medication, and new feelings of control, hope, and education helped her form new ideas about herself that told her this was not about her character; even so, the self-distortion did not go away that easily. She needed to do more work. The medication and education would help her continue with this work, instead of being an end in themselves.

In Journey Two, now that she was able to see her situation clearly because of medication, therapy, and the support from her AD/HD group, Jennifer began to feel she didn't deserve to be treated this way. Even though she still had many AD/HD challenges, she also felt secure enough about herself and less vulnerable enough that she agreed to get some other types of support, hiring baby-sitting and cleaning help so she had more energy to put toward new experiences that continued to enhance her self-concept.

As she began to have new experiences of herself, Jennifer's self-distortion decreased. She put herself in situations where more people could appreciate her. For example, when she began to do some volunteer work at a senior center, Jennifer started to get new feedback from other people and to see herself in a new way. They thought her arts-and-crafts projects were very interesting and stimulating. They listened to her with a respect that was not based entirely on how well she was managing her household. Eventually, she began to respect herself and internalize this other part of the picture of herself.

Jennifer went through a long period of growth and development as her self-view and perspective on her life changed. At some point she was able to see herself as a complete person, even though she still had difficulties. Her good feelings about herself were more solidified and no longer as dependent on other people's good view of her.

As a result, she was able to tell her husband when she was feeling angry in response to his negative characterizations of her. Since she no longer bought into his view of her, she could set limits with him and protect herself in a healthy way.

After so many years feeling she deserved her husband's occasional mean-spirited attacks, one day something changed. "Last night, he blew up at me again," she reported to me. "But this time, I didn't feel it in the same way." She had been in her quiet sanctuary of a converted spare room, which she had fixed up with the help of a professional organizer. She was doing yoga, a newly acquired habit that helped focus and relax her. When her husband started slamming cupboard doors downstairs in the kitchen, Jennifer realized she must have left them open. A few minutes later, he pushed open the door to her quiet room and started yelling about how they were supposed to be at a close friend's for a dinner party in fifteen minutes. Jennifer had totally forgotten. Not only that, she had forgotten to clean up the mess in the kitchen. Her husband called her an "irresponsible selfish slob," said he was "fed up living like this," and ended the tirade with: "What kind of mother are you, anyway?"

"This time, though," she told me, "instead of falling apart inside, and just standing there till he was finished, I felt myself sort of observe the whole thing instead of being lost in it. It was amazing. I just said I was sorry I forgot about the party, that I knew he was frustrated about that as well as the mess in the kitchen, and that I would go get ready, *but* that I wasn't going to stand here and listen to his tirade. I told him it made me angry to have him go off like that—we certainly had difficulties to deal with, but not like this, and that despite all the problems I have, he is not to talk to me like that. So I just went to the bedroom and got ready," she said. "It was the first time I ever walked away from him when he was going off like that."

Jennifer's ability to set limits (with her husband) and to walk away when his attacks became personal showed me that she was beginning to separate out the way she needed to be treated in a relationship from her difficulties with AD/HD. She no longer felt that she deserved toxic treatment. Her core sense of self was no longer synonymous with her primary AD/HD symptoms. Jennifer would need to keep working on strategies for remembering appointments with her husband, and they would have to continue to talk about and validate his rights and feelings at a later time when their communication could be effective. But Jennifer no longer felt trapped by her own belief that she needed to absorb any and all personal attacks because of her difficulties.

By Journey Three, when Jennifer began to have a life outside her family and her AD/HD difficulties, she became far more independent. Though her husband and children were still the largest, most important part of her life, they now had to share her with others. Her husband, in particular, felt a loss of control. He was happy that she felt better about herself and was more vital and even more effective as a wife and mother. On the other hand, she was around the house less and he could not help but feel that she needed him less and that he was now less important to her.

The response of Jennifer's family to her busier schedule was subtle and unconscious, as change-back messages often are. When Jennifer arrived home from coffee with friends, yoga class, or an afternoon of volunteer work, her children and husband barely seemed to notice her. They went on with life as though she were not there. Of course, for Jennifer, who feared insignificance, this subtle message to return to her former ways was particularly powerful and tempting. But now, because of her support, medication, and her changing perception of herself, she was able to withstand this temptation and continue on with her expanded life until the whole family began to see her and the family dynamic differently. In order to reach this point, where she protected herself but still connected with her family, where she was able to remain herself and be in the family in a more satisfying way, Jennifer had to confront many psychological barriers and family rules, as discussed in previous chapters.

Don Comes Out of Hiding

After his initial treatment for primary symptoms, Don continued to try to fit in and hide his differences at work. Inside he felt unsatisfied, unfulfilled, and inauthentic. At the start of Journey One, he focused all his efforts on hiding his difficulties, overcompensating in those areas to the detriment of all the rest of his interests and talents.

At work, an employee supervised by Don was falling down on his sales and losing customers. When Don attempted to discuss this serious situation with him, though, the employee would begin to joke about Don's messy, unorganized office, in some way discrediting Don's right to have such a conversation. At this early point, Don kept quiet about the employee's problems since Don himself bought into this reasoning.

For years, Don was known in his company as a "softy"—a supervisor employees could take advantage of. He was too easy on those he supervised because he had placed himself in a one-down position with them; he felt that he could hardly ask them to come on time to meetings, observe deadlines, and keep their work spaces organized when he had problems in these areas himself.

In Journey Two, with support, Don was able to shift some of his focus to his other talents and abilities that he had suppressed in early adulthood when he became more overwhelmed with his AD/HD difficulties and differences. He now had a new yardstick with which to measure himself. In the safe environment of an AD/HD group, he was able to be seen again, and accepted and respected. He felt encouraged to slowly make his way to other groups, especially to the poetry group where he rediscovered his true passion.

After he began developing his self-concept, Don was able to distinguish between his AD/HD and his right and obligation as a supervisor to ensure that his employees delivered quality work. To make this distinction, he had to overcome his feeling that his own AD/HD took away his authority or rights. He was able to see his organizational problems in their proper perspective, and he could internalize a much different feeling about himself, one that wasn't completely dependent on whether he had deficits. He was now able to maintain his sense of self, perspective, and self-respect, even in the face of his struggle.

In Journey Three Don needed to learn how to handle the new success that came his way and had to confront his fear that setting limits would make his success and others' goodwill toward him vanish. He began to feel comfortable enough to give of himself to others in order to form real relationships. And he felt empowered enough to shift the power balance at work to maintain his position of respect, even while coping with his difficulties.

This new unique persona that he was able to show to others at work actually made Don more interesting. Rather than thinking him weird, when Don revealed his poetic side, some of the guys thought they were boring by comparison. They actually came to respect him, and he had a breakthrough in connection by letting people know who he really was.

By revealing who he was, he attracted others to him with whom he shared some of the same interests, talents, and feelings about the company—other people who had been hiding various aspects of themselves since they felt different too.

Beth's Talents Shine Through

Whereas Don's trigger was feeling weird and Jennifer's was feeling insignificant, Beth's trigger was being seen as messy. She would do anything to keep people from calling her that.

In Journey One she tried to hide her "differentness" and mistakenly attributed her problems with relationships to AD/HD rather than to her own secretiveness. She kept men at a distance to protect herself, to avoid revealing to them her messiness. A common way that adults with AD/HD deal with their differences in relationships early on in their journeys is to withdraw from others. Ironically, adults who withdraw or hide themselves do so out of the belief that their differences, if seen, will drive others away. What often ends up happening, however, is that they chase other people away when they withdraw.

In Journey Two Beth was able to start having new experiences of herself. She actually started meeting other creative people and realized that they shared many of her traits. She began to put the messy label in proper perspective, so that the thought of someone calling her messy or seeing this side of her didn't send her running for safety. It just became part of what she needed to deal with in life, but not the whole picture anymore.

In Journey Three Beth was now in a position to give

more, as well as to consider her own needs and ask for them to be met. By the end of Journey Three, she realized she was not just Messy Bethie anymore. She was a talented, creative woman who also had organizational difficulties. The judgmental feelings had not been coming from men but from inside herself. She was eventually able to disclose her difficulties and ask for her needs and differences to be addressed, using the communication model that we discussed in the preceding chapter.

When she learned to communicate in a way that allowed her to maintain protection but still reveal herself, when she found a better fit for herself personally and professionally, she was making the changes that would lead to more satisfaction in life, even though she still struggled with AD/HD symptoms.

Lance Makes Better Choices

Unlike the others, who needed to be less focused on their deficits, Lance's challenge was to learn to be more realistic about the impact his difficulties were having on his life. In Journey Two he needed to develop a more complete picture of himself, instead of seeing just the strengths on which he had gotten by for years.

After treatment with medication and education about AD/HD, Lance was able to focus on doing more of what he wanted to do, which was usually more than he could handle. He had to do a great deal of inner work before he could feel comfortable enough to get support to make up for his difficulty with the executive function of his brain.

It took him several years, and many crises in business

and relationships and many consultations with AD/HD specialists, before he got to the point of understanding that he had to allow himself to really "get" how much his deficits were interfering with his strengths and his goals. In Journey Two he started to experiment with support and began to have a vision of a new way of life that wasn't so crisis-oriented, while still being exciting and stimulating.

In Journey Three Lance's challenge was to make choices that kept him challenged but with some kind of built-in containment of his impulse to dive headfirst into exciting new creative endeavors. His goal was to build a new positive cycle where he was able to manage his deficits in order to support his strengths so he could be more consistently successful and not repeatedly disappoint others. This took him a long time, but with the support of an AD/HD group that gave him honest feedback, he was eventually able to reach his goal and make better choices. Because so many good opportunities came his way, Lance would need to be vigilant to maintain his support and stay on track. To manage his life and have satisfying relationships, he would have to turn down *some* good opportunities, based on his inner criteria.

All of these stories illustrate how internal growth can eventually lead to overall improvements in life satisfaction. The reduction of primary symptoms doesn't always correspond with these inner changes and may not occur until some of these other changes have taken place. Internal growth is a complex process in the voyage toward wholeness—where your strengths and weaknesses come together, where the past, present, and future become connected through a new

In your journeys through AD/HD, you need to have the right signposts leading you to the desired destinations. This is the framework I have provided in this book. You need sufficient fuel (your medication) and a well-running vehicle (your brain) that you know how to operate.

Especially on a voyage through difficult terrain, like this one, it is good to have a guide, such as a coach or a therapist or another experienced traveler who's been there and knows both the obstacles and the rewards along the way.

Don't worry about whether you "are there yet." The entire voyage takes a lifetime.

understanding and identity. Eventually, new dreams are born, and you can give this gift of who you are and how you are different to others, thereby enriching their lives and your relationship with them.

Appendix A
Guides to Portable Travel

Emergency Kit

Make a photocopy of the SAFETY model and Bill of Rights. Keep them in your pocket or purse for emergency communication situations such as when encountering toxic help. *Remember:* Your worth is separate from your AD/HD problems. Describe what you need or what happened; don't characterize yourself.

SAFETY Review Model

S   **Separate**

A   **AD/HD from your your core sense of self**

F   **Figure out what you need.**

E   **Express your understanding and appreciation of the other person.**

T   **Tell the other person about your difficulty and your need.**

Y   **You give suggestions.**

AD/HD Bill of Rights in Partnerships

- **Even though you have AD/HD, you have the right to get angry at your partner.**

- **Even though you have AD/HD, you have the right to be treated as an equal and competent partner. You don't have to give up power because of AD/HD.**

- **Even though you need that help doesn't mean you need to:**

- **Relinquish control or respect—you can still set limits.**

- **Give up responsibility for knowing what's going on or getting things done even by delegating.**

Journal for Your Trip

Use the following questions as a guide to record and reflect your daily experiences on the trip.

- **What emotional pangs did I notice today? What triggers? Are these clues to what I must do next?**

- **What feelings about differences did I notice?**

- **What went well today? Why? How can I make this happen more regularly?**

- **What strengths have I focused on today?**

- At what point did I feel most authentically myself? What experiences can I have to bring me more of these feelings?

- What deficit did I focus on too much and allow to detract from my overall sense of self-worth?

- Where did I give up power in relationships because of difficulties?

- Where did I show my uniqueness? And in what way?

- How did I ask for or accept help?

- What limits did I set?

- How did I connect with someone?

- How do I protect my emotional needs?

- What did I do when I felt overwhelmed?

- Did I have any fears or avoid anything because of possible false negative expectations?

Aids for Organizing Your Life

These products, services, and strategies can help you organize your activities, commitments, surroundings, and your
time in different ways as yu progress through your journeys.

Do It Yourself

- **Post-it notes**
- **Planners**
- **Time- and clutter-management courses**
- **Beepers and buzzers**

Get Help from Others

Professional Help

- **Professional organizers**
- **Housecleaners and housekeepers**
- **Baby-sitters**
- **Coaches**
- **Assistants**

Personal Support

- **Trading jobs**
- **Buddy systems**
- **Support groups**

Find the Right Balance

Learn to reduce or increase the following variables to create just the right balance. Do you know how to manipulate these factors for yourself?

- **Time**
- **Support**
- **Structure**
- **Number of variables**
- **Degree of difficulty**
- **Degree of distractibility**
- **Degree of stimulation**
- **Medication**
- **Stress, rest, emotions involved**
- **Degree of control possible**

Other Strategies That Modify the Variables:

- **Simplifying**
- **Cutting down**
- **Cutting out**
- **Adding more support**
- **Adding structure**
- **Accommodating for difficulties**
- **Sharing**
- **Modifying the environment**
- **Utilizing regular and consistent support, assistance, and partnership to fill in your gaps**

Create New Space (Physical, Time, or Psychological) for Yourself

- More rest, relaxation, relationships, renewal.

- More time spent in areas of strengths than deficits.

Hone Your Communications Skills

- Let people get closer to you.
- Ask for help when you need it.
- Describe what you need.
- Set limits.
- Say no to others when that's what's best for yourself.
- Say yes to you.
- Confront fear of conflict, fear of change.
- Strive for a balance of power in your relationships.

Use Your Own Sense of Self as an Organizing Principle

- Define a clear sense of self; know your own limits, strengths, values, and beliefs.

- Let your inner voice be the strongest stimulus in your environment.

- Instead of being bombarded with the external pulls and overload of everyone else's demands and agendas, use your sense of self as a guide to finding a good fit in your relationships and your work.

- Your internal sense of self ultimately leads to internal organization, which brings an increased sense of control and choice.

Appendix B
Tools for Mental Health Professionals (and the Adults Who Work with Them)

Intervention Guide

This guide will help professionals assess their clients' difficulties and to determine where the emphasis needs to be placed during treatment. It can also serve as a springboard for discussions with clients, as well as a review of the journeys discussed in this book.

Journey One
Focus: The Brain
Crisis of Understanding

Journey Two
Focus: The Self
Crisis of Identity

Journey Three
Focus: Your Self in the World
Crisis of Success

I. Organizing

Journey One

- Uses external measures
- Organizes alone, with no outside support
- Uses exclusively external aids, such as beepers and planners
- Support just beginning to be considered but is often resisted

Journey Two

- Better able to utilize physical support like professional organizers
- Asks for help more easily

Journey Three

- Begins to learn to organize life from within based on meaning and value
- Learns how to operate brain well in order to organize life more effectively
- Inner voice becomes a signal that provides a strong organizing principle

II. Strategies Used for Control of Primary Symptoms

Journey One

- Resists medication or takes medication as exclusive approach
- Embarks on education about the brain and AD/HD
- May attend conferences or presentations

Journey Two

- Takes medication as part of a larger plan
- May join a support group
- Attends conferences
- More willing to ask for accommodations

Journey Three

- Know personal optimal conditions for functioning
- Continually readjust variables to maximize effectiveness of strategies
- Counseling or coaching can help ensure continual progress and overcome internal barriers

III. View of Differences and Self

Journey One

- Begins to understand why they have felt different all their lives
- Still hides difficulties and differences a great deal
- Focuses on deficits
- Devalues self because of deficits or distorts self-image
- Stuck in negative feedback loop
- Defines self by AD/HD
- Ashamed of differences
- Sees self as defective

Journey Two

- Expands and corrects distorted self-view
- Affiliates more with others with AD/HD
- Begins to let in new data about self
- Reverses negative feedback loop to some extent and begins positive one
- Begins to value differences
- Develops differences
- Core sense of self separates from AD/HD
- Counseling for self-image and expectations possible now
- Lets self be seen by others more

Journey Three

- Able to give differences as gift to be really known—even with difficulties
- Able to connect with others rather than hide
- Sees self as unique, not defective

IV. Acceptance

Journey One

- Judges success exclusively by external measures
- Hope and relief at diagnosis
- Grief cycle begins to be worked through
- Pseudo-acceptance—resigned or intent on getting over AD/HD

- Acceptance of the fact of AD/HD but not the self with it—wants to get over who they are
- Incomplete grief cycle
- Will resist shift of original vision to something that fits better

Journey Two

- Learns to get on with life anyway—even with symptoms persisting
- Reaches deeper acceptance of self and life with AD/HD
- Better able to shift energies into areas that are better fits

Journey Three

- Able to assess success from inside
- Accepts that goal is to be more of self, not less
- Can maintain sense of self in face of negative judgments

V. Balance in Life

Journey One

- Spends most time and energy in areas of deficits
- Overwhelmed by them

Journey Two

- Begins to be able to have more recreation, relaxation, relationships—even when difficulties persist
- Focuses on strengths and deficits more equally

Journey Three

- Overwhelmed by choices that are created by working in areas of strengths
- Needs to develop criteria for choices

VI. Identity, Meaning, and Authenticity

Journey One

- Afraid to examine pain of old dreams
- Afraid to dream again

Journey Two

- Examines pain of lost dreams
- Faces an identity crisis
- Sense of vitality and authenticity returns
- Begins to live in unique zone, showing more fully who they really are
- Crisis of "Who am I now?"
- Examines pain, forms a new vision; a new identity solidifying
- Growing sense of authenticity, meaning, energy, vitality

Journey Three

- Able to maintain new sense of self in relationships—even when feeling different

VII. Relationships, Communication, Intimacy

Journey One

- Withdraws when AD/HD embarrasses

- Won't communicate needs

- Overprotects or overconnects

- Stays in inferior positions in
  relationships and toxic relationships
  because of AD/HD

Journey Two

- Spends more time with people who can
  see and value all of them

- Able to ask for help without sacrificing
  self-respect

Journey Three

- Begins to be able to confront psychological and family barriers to restructuring
  their life

- Learns to communicate to both connect
  and protect

- Begins to be able to let self be known

- Rebalances power dynamics

- Sets limits and boundaries

- Able to validate the other person

- Able to be assertive in communication about AD/HD

- Able to express needs and differences

Markers of Success

- Assesses progress from inner state, not only from observable AD/HD symptoms

- Moves toward a healthier self-image and a more authentic, fulfilled life

- Feels more in control

- Feels more satisfaction

- Uses strengths more of the time

- Able to both connect and protect

- Able to see both sides of self at same time

- Separates core self from AD/HD

- Knows what is needed in order to operate well and is able to ask for it

- Knows how to make decisions and organize life from values and around meaning

Thirty Questions to Ask

Professionals can explore these questions with their clients, and adults with AD/HD can use them for self-assessment. The questions are a tool for assessing treatment progress and planning goals for treatment.

1. **Where is the focus of their lives now? Before? Can they operate in their areas of strengths?**

Are they spending more of their time operating in these areas?

2. How do they view themselves and their differences now? Before? Do they hide, value, understand, develop, or protect them? Give examples.

3. How do they think about their symptoms in relation to themselves? In relationships?

4. Are they more resilient now? More accurate in their assessments of themselves and others?

5. Do they get support when they need it? Do they know what they need support for? Are they getting the right support?

6. How have they handled their primary AD/HD symptoms? What still needs adjusting? Consider: medications, education, self-image, connections with others, support—organizing, coaching, accommodations, counseling (couples, careers), and other help.

7. Are they getting all their biological needs taken care of?

8. Can they set limits in the face of toxic help? Can they keep their self-concept separate from their AD/HD? Can they maintain their sense of self with others?

9. Can they use their uniqueness in the world?

10. Do they have an accurate view of the long-term voyage, or are they waiting to be "cured"? How are they evaluating success?

11. Are they waiting to be understood completely in relationships?

12. Are they in situations where they can be seen? How can they build competence and confidence?

13. Are they connected to others with AD/HD with whom they can identify and connect? Do they have role models of uniqueness?

14. Can they communicate while validating other people?

15. Are they excited about possibilities?

16. Are they overwhelmed? If so, by deficits or by strengths?

17. Can they organize their life in internal ways?

18. What has happened regarding their ability to make good choices for their lives and for who they are? How has it changed?

19. Do they accept themselves and their life with AD/HD? Are they resigned to give up their dreams? Are they intent on getting over AD/HD? What boundary can they set to change things?

20. Do they keep having the same negative experience of self? What choices lead to this?

21. What's scary about examining their past dreams?

22. What power in their relationships have they given up because of their differences?

23. What new experience might they need in order to correct their self-image?

24. Do they overconnect or overprotect? With what results?

25. **What deficit do they focus too much attention on?**

26. **When did they first realize they had differences?**

27. **Do they have the freedom to make new and better choices?**

28. **Do they have the ability and knowledge to make good choices?**

29. **Do they have a new way to interpret experiences to themselves?**

30. **Do they feel a new sense of vitality and authenticity?**

Counseling for the Rest of the Voyage

The treatment of ADD should never overlook that the patient is a person first and a person with ADD second.
—Edward Hallowell, M.D., in Kathleen G. Nadeau, ed.,
A Comprehensive Guide to Attention Deficit Disorder in Adults

All these years the "real" self of adults coping with the challenges of Attention Deficit/Hyperactivity Disorder may have been hidden away under their symptoms. At some point after diagnosis and initial treatment, all the tools of medication, education, and counseling can be used in support of the search for self that now must take center stage. After the beginning search for information about the brain and AD/HD comes the search for who an individual is becoming as a result of these new tools and information.

Professionals must keep up with the changing needs of

these adults. We must not be lulled into assuming, when we see people doing well after that initial treatment, that they are cured, or that treating the primary symptoms will be the end of the story. We must understand the voyage in order to provide guidelines; we should help steer the course so that adults can choose experiences in and out of therapy that will have a positive effect on their self-view and their differences.

Professionals must be aware, even if they have successfully assisted these adults early on, that the emphasis must shift at some point from the science of medication and adjusting the brain to the complex inner and lifelong task of living with differences.

The Counselor Guide

A knowledgeable AD/HD counselor can be a critical link and must convey a sense of sureness about the path. The therapist in this situation may be the first significant person to understand the voyage, to give some kind of explanations back to the client. Unless the client trusts that the therapist understands the voyage, he or she will not feel comfortable enough to let go of old distortions and false beliefs, fearing there will be nothing with which to replace them.

New Dreams

At some point in the counseling process, the counselor can facilitate the emerging pain of past losses and help clients

> *When we are dreaming alone it is only dreaming. When we are dreaming with others it is the beginning of reality.*
>
> — author unknown

bring together the past, present, and future in a new vision that brings them closer to expressing who they are at a particular time. Some coaches play this role as well. Hope Langner, a coach with Coaches Training Institute, says, "[My clients] work with me to discover their unique selves, to live their lives expressing who they really are." She goes on to say that this kind of coaching focuses on helping clients discover "what they really want, follow through on plans and goals, stay on target even when the going gets tough, and, most importantly, find and listen to their voice."

Treatment in any form—coaching or counseling, or self-help or support groups—must take a longer and deeper view of its long-term goals from the beginning. These goals are the continued growth toward meaning, and purpose, a newly awakened sense of passion about life, and the eventual integration of the AD/HD identity with the past passion in order to move forward into the future with renewed vitality and vision.

Many of my clients, after beginning to see themselves more clearly, still report their successes at work or at home with a flat tone; but when they told me about the dreams they once had, I could see a new light in their eyes. This sense of aliveness is crucial and cannot be ignored in the treatment of adults with AD/HD.

The Importance of the Therapeutic Relationship

Therapy is obviously a situation where a person can have the experience of being seen and can feel more comfortable revealing one's self. It is especially helpful for people who have the most difficulty seeing themselves clearly, and for people who don't yet have other opportunities for this in their life. It is helpful for those who aren't willing to let in other positive reflections because they feel they just don't deserve it or they are not yet willing to risk it. Therapists can provide a supportive "holding environment" until a person is able to hold on to this expanded self-view, to see it and not let it slip away with the first negative experience.

The healing and critical role played by a therapist who understands these issues, and respects the complexities and difficulties of living with these differences, is often underestimated in the long-term treatment of adults with AD/HD. And the importance of a therapeutic relationship in the overall treatment of adult AD/HD is often overlooked or undervalued. It is critical, though, because it is usually the first accepting relationship with a significant person the adult with AD/HD may have ever had.

Kevin Murphy addresses this point in *A Comprehensive Guide to Attention Deficit Disorder in Adults*, edited by Kathleen G. Nadeau: "Those professionals working with adults with ADD need to help counteract the ingrained negative self perceptions to create conditions that empower patients to believe their lives can be different and activate them to engage in and persist with treatment. Instilling hope, fostering in patients a belief that they are potent and can succeed, and demonstrating a sincere and ongoing commitment to helping patients work around their difficulties appear to be important and sometimes overlooked components of treatment for adults with ADD." (p. 144).

Many times the client's focus is only on getting over AD/HD and concentrating on deficits. It is the therapist's responsibility not to allow the sessions to go in this direction. Otherwise the client will easily be depleted and demoralized about his or her progress.

The therapist may be the only individual in the person's life who has ever steadfastly held on to the whole picture for the client, seeing both strengths and weaknesses. This is significant because the individual's self-view at this point easily slips away when AD/HD episodes occur.

Treatment Basics at a Glance

- **Always start with the brain and the primary symptoms. Always start with it and go back to it.**

- **Counseling must be collaborative and interactive.**

- **Don't assign any step to be taken between sessions or accept a client's suggestions without exploring the intersection of AD/HD and psychology.**

- **An individual is ready to leave counseling when he or she:**

  - **has developed an internal valuing and explanatory voice;**

  - **is able to get support outside of counselors and professionals;**

  - **has the ability to make good personal choices.**

The first item is particularly important. Remember, the point of all this is to improve functioning. So go as far as you can; then stop when you hit an inner barrier and explore what prevents your client from taking the next step. Discuss: "What would be difficult about taking this step? What do you think would happen if you took it?" Sometimes it's impaired executive functioning itself or a missing cognitive piece that is preventing someone from taking the next step, and sometimes it's a psychological barrier. Analyze the stumbling block until you both understand it.

Some Ineffective and Problematic Treatments

Here are three common approaches to treating AD/HD in adults that aren't always the most effective ways of dealing with the problem. These kinds of approaches often fall short or lead the individual off course, in pursuit of a counterproductive goal.

"Take This Pill Today and Clean Your House in the Morning"

I know of someone who was actually given medication, told to take these pills, and "when your house is clean, you'll know you are cured." This advice obviously is problematic because it is not true that:

- **medication is a cure.**

- **the point of AD/HD treatment is to be cured.**

- **medication is a magic pill for housecleaning.**

Most advice is not so blatantly off course, but messages such as "you must be cured of yourself," or that the only criterion for success is "how clean your house is" or "how organized you are," lead many people off course for a long time. It leaves them feeling worse about themselves as time goes on, that they are failing again, even after diagnosis and treatment.

It also reinforces to families that this is the goal of treatment, instead of bringing the family together to understand more deeply and completely who this individual is and what the ongoing challenges of an AD/HD life are.

Give That Man a Cookie

A therapist said to his client, an attorney with AD/HD, "If you're on time every day this week to work (or court), I'll have a chocolate chip cookie waiting for you." (The client loved chocolate-chip cookies.) Don't treat adults with AD/HD as if they were children! This attempt at behavioral modification was insulting and degrading to the client.

There should be a respectful partnership between the therapist and the client with AD/HD, not an authoritative or parental one. As author and psychiatrist Edward Hallowell writes in Nadeau's *Comprehensive Guide*: "While some of the child literature can be applied to adults such as need for external structure, the nature of the day to day difficulties that an adult with ADD experiences is vastly different from that of a child. When treating adults it is also necessary to keep in mind that they are carrying with them years of ingrained behavior patterns and a reinforced negative self image that can initially block the path to change" (p. 146).

Keep Your Nose to the Grindstone

Another problem exists when clients, with the encouragement of the therapist, repeatedly try and repeatedly fail to follow a rigid schedule. They often will feel suffocated very quickly or try to motivate themselves by using negative re-inforcement. I have seen this many times, and believe me, it doesn't work any more than a starvation diet does for effective weight control.

Avoiding Reinjury

Right from the start the counselor needs to have acceptance and understanding of differences. Just as counselors need to recognize and respect how different cultural groups may perceive eye contact, touch, and so forth, they need to respect and not misinterpret adults with AD/HD who may interrupt, want to take notes, or tape sessions, arrive late, or forget what happened during the previous session.

All these behaviors should be taken in the proper context. That's not to say that people with AD/HD can't be displaying the same resistance to therapy as anyone else. A practitioner needs to be able to figure out whether a particular behavior is neurological or psychological in nature and to engage with the client to problem-solve in the right way.

Working with Other AD/HD Professional Helpers

Working with professional coaches, organizers, or tutors often brings up powerful feelings (such as shame or embarrassment) for adults with AD/HD since this experience reminds them of earlier traumatic situations of failure. I've known clients to lie to coaches rather than feel the shame triggered by disappointing others, or they take months to make a call to an organizer because shame keeps them from letting someone close enough to see vulnerable areas. These supports need to be added in the proper sequence; otherwise the individual often hits barriers that prevent effective working relationships. This can result in premature termination of these critical supports.

Preparing for these other supports in a safe therapeutic relationship by first expanding one's self-concept allows clients to eventually take full advantage of them and to transfer the skills that they acquire to real-life situations. When one's self-concept is expanded, when one sees the self as larger than one's AD/HD difficulties and is less vulnerable to past hurts, performance-oriented services aren't as threatening.

The differences and boundaries between AD/HD coaching and counseling often get cloudy. It's often a good idea for the client to work with both a counselor and coach who are open to coordination efforts and maintaining boundaries. An effective AD/HD counselor is able to move back and forth effectively between counseling and coaching the client but will recommend that the client use the services of a coach when support is needed on a more frequent basis. Likewise, an AD/HD coach will need to refer the client back to the mental health professional to work through the emotions surrounding the AD/HD issues when they arise or present barriers.

I asked Susan Sussman and Nancy Ratey, pioneers in the field of AD/HD coaching, to clarify and describe what to look for in AD/HD coaching. They say that "individuals with AD/HD often know what changes they want to make in their lives, but don't always know how to make those changes. And most importantly, they can get distracted from their goals. The coach can be instrumental in starting an ongoing process of defining long-range goals and short-term objectives, and in keeping the individual on the defined path once it becomes clear. Many individuals with AD/HD also use a coach to help them assess their strengths and weaknesses, learn how to compensate for weaknesses, and develop personal styles that draw on their strengths. "AD/HD coaching is a collaborative process. It uses a process of inquiry to assist clients in maximizing their strengths and talents and taking action toward the realization of their goals. AD/HD coaching helps clients understand themselves and their disability, develop the structure needed to function successfully, and become powerful self-advocates.

"The client and the coach work as a team to identify areas of difficulty and develop strategies for overcoming them. The client agrees to become accountable for his or her time and actions, and the coach agrees to hold the client accountable. The coach is flexible and can work with the client in person, by telephone, fax or an on-line service, in an office, at the client's home, or at the client's work site. The coach is amenable to working alone or in a team with the client's psychotherapist, physician, and/or work-site personnel.

"Before contacting an AD/HD coach, a potential client should have a clear picture of what he or she wants and needs from the coaching relationship. Clients' needs vary tremendously. Similarly, coaches often choose to specialize in specific areas. For example, coaches may specialize in

> Patients must feel the clinician is a partner with them who also sincerely believes they can be helped. The human element in clinician interactions with patients should never be underestimated.
>
> —Kevin Murphy, in Kathleen G. Nadeau, ed.,
> *A Comprehensive Guide to Attention Deficit*
> *Disorder in Adults*

time management, organizing in the home and/or office, clutter control, or budgeting. Therefore, finding a good client–coach match is in large part a result of how well the client is able to articulate his or her needs. The client should also take into account the coach's training, style, goals, and method of delivering services."

Recommended Resources

AD/HD

Books

Adamec, Christine A. *Moms with ADD: A Self-Help Manual*. Dallas, Tex.: Taylor Trade Publishing, 2000.

Amen, Daniel G., M.D. *Healing ADD: The Breakthrough Program That Allows You to See and Heal the Six Types of Attention Deficit Disorder*. New York: G.P. Putnam's Sons, 2001.

Bramer, Jennifer. *Succeeding in College with Attention Deficit Disorders*. Plantation, Fla.: Specialty Press, 1996.

Fellman, Wilma R. *Finding a Career That Works for You*. Plantation, Fla.: Specialty Press, 2000.

Hallowell, Edward, M.D., and John Ratey, M.D. *Answers to Distraction*. New York: Pantheon Books, 1995.

_____. *Driven to Distraction*. New York: Pantheon Books, 1994.

Halverstadt, Jonathan Scott. *ADD & Romance: Finding Fulfillment in Love, Sex, & Relationships*. Dallas, TX: Taylor Trade Publishing, 1999.

Hartmann, Thomas. *ADD Success Stories*. Grass Valley, Calif.: Underwood Books, 1992.

_____. *Attention Deficit Disorder: A Different Perception*. Grass Valley, Calif.: Underwood Books, 1993; revised 1997.

Katz, Mark. *On Playing a Poor Hand Well: Insights from the Lives of Those Who Have Overcome Childhood Risks and Adversities*. New York: Norton, 1997.

Kelly, Kate, and Peggy Ramundo. *You Mean I'm Not Lazy, Stupid, or Crazy?!* Cincinnati, Ohio: Scribner, 1995.

Kelly, Kate, Peggy Ramundo, and D. Steven Ledingham. *The ADDed Dimension: Everyday Advice for Adults with ADD*. New York: Scribner, 1997.

Latham, P., and P. Latham. *Attention Deficit Disorder and the Law: A Guide for Advocates,*. Washington, D.C.: JKL Communications, 1992.

Murphy, Kevin R., and Suzanne Levert. *Out of the Fog: Treatment Options and Coping Strategies for Adult Attention Deficit Disorder.* New York: Hyperion/Skylight Press, 1995.

Nadeau, Kathleen, Ellen Littman, and Patricia Quinn, M.D. *Understanding Girls with AD/HD.* Silver Spring, Md.: Advantage Books, 1999.

Nadeau, Kathleen G. and Patricia Quinn, M.D. *Understanding Women with AD/HD.* Silver Spring, MD: Advantage Books, 2002.

Nadeau, Kathleen G. *ADD in the Workplace: Choices, Changes, & Challenges.* New York: Brunner/Mazel, 1996.

_____, *Adventures in Fast Forward: Life, Love and Work for the ADD Adult.* New York: Brunner/Mazel, 1996.

_____, ed. *A Comprehensive Guide to Attention Deficit Disorder in Adults.* New York: Brunner/Mazel, 1995.

Novotni, Michele, with Randy Petersen. *What Does Everybody Else Know That I Don't?* Plantation, Fla.: Specialty Press, 1999.

Quinn, Pat, Nancy Ratey, and Theresa Maitlan. *Coaching College Students with ADHD: Issues & Answers.* Betheseda, Md.: Advantage Books, 2000. (To order, call 888-238-8588.)

Richardson, Wendy. *The Link Between ADD and Addiction: Getting the Help You Deserve.* Colorado Springs, Colo.: Pinon Press, 1997.

Solden, Sari. *Women with Attention Deficit Disorder.* Grass Valley, Calif.: Underwood Books, 1995.

Weiss, Lynn. *ADD and Creativity: Taping Your Inner Muse.* Dallas, Tex.: Taylor Publishing, 1996.

_____, *ADD on the Job.* Dallas, Tex.: Taylor Publishing, 1996.

Whiteman, Thomas A., and Michele Novotni. *Adult ADD.* Colorado Springs, Colo.: Pinon Press, 1995.

Audiovisual Materials

Outside In: A Look at Adults With Attention Deficit Disorder. Glencoe, Ill.: Family Today, 1999. Videocassette.

Copps, Steven. *Twice as Hard for Half as Much.* Atlanta, Ga: ADDA 2000 National Conference. Videocasette. (Order through Chesapeake Audio/Video, 410-796-0040 or e-mail cavc@mind-spring.com.)

Solden, Sari. *Women with Attention Deficit Disorder*. Ann Arbor, Mich.: Frontier Publishing, 1995. Audiotape. (Order through Web site www.sarisolden.com.)

Stanford, Paula, and Becky Stanford. *Dismissed and Undiagnosed Dreamers*. Oklahoma City, Okla.: Paula Stanford Human Resource Network, 1997. Videocassette. (To order, call 405-943-5073.)

Catalogs, Magazines, and Newsletters

ADDitude
ADDitude Foundation, Inc.
P.O. Box 421
2476 Bolsover
Houston, TX 77005-2518
Phone: 800-856-2032
Web site: www.additudemag.com

ADD Warehouse Catalog
300 Northwest Seventieth Avenue,
Suite 102
Plantation, FL 33317
Phone: 954-792-8944
Web site: www.addwarehouse.com

The ADHD Challenge
P.O. Box 2277
West Peabody, MA 01960-7277
Phone: 800-ADD-2332
Fax: 978-53-LEARN

The ADHD Report
Guilford Publications, Inc.
72 Spring Street
New York, NY 10012
Phone: 800-365-7006

ADD Information Exchange Network (ADDIEN)
P.O. Box 1991
Ann Arbor, MI 48106-1991
Phone: 734-426-1659
Fax: 734-426-0116
Web site: www.addien.org
E-mail: addien@aol.com

Children and Adults with Attention Deficit Disorder (CHADD)
8181 Professional Place, Suite 201
Landover, MD 20785
Phone: 800-233-4050 or 301-306-7070
Fax: 301-306-7090
Web site: www.chadd.org
(Members receive *Attention* Magazine)

Kitty Petty ADD/LD Institute
410 Sheridan Avenue, Suite 339
Palo Alto, CA 94306-2020
Phone: 650-329-9443
Fax: 650-321-5939
Web site: www.kpinst.org
E-mail: kitty@kpinst.org

National Attention Deficit Disorder Association
1788 Second Street, Suite 200
Highland Park, IL 60035
Phone: 847-432-2332
Fax: 847-432-5874
Web site: www.add.org
E-mail: mail@add.org
(Members receive *Focus* Magazine)

Seminars and Retreats

RENEWAL
P.O. Box 154
Slingerlands, NY 12159
Phone: 518-448-5868
E-mail: RenewalADD@aol.com

Other Web Sites

www.addvance.com
www.add.about.com
www.ADDconsults.com
www.adders.org (United Kingdom and other countries)
www.addult.org/
www.ADHD.com
www.adhdnews.com
www.sarisolden.com (discussion forum)
www.thomhartmann.com
www.drhallowell.com

Organizing Your Life

Books

Covey, Stephen R., A. Roger Merill, and Rebecca R. Merrill. *First Things First: To Live, To Love, To Learn, To Leave a Legacy.* New York: Fireside, 1996.

Felton, Sandra. *The New Messies Manual.* Grand Rapids, Mich.: Fleming N. Revell, 2000.

Glovinsky, Cindy. *Making Peace with the Things in Your Life.* New York: St. Martin's Press, 2002.

Kolberg, Judith. *Conquering Chronic Disorganization.* DeCatur, Ga.: Squall Press, 1999.

Kolberg, Judith, and Kathleen G. Nadeau, Ph.D. *ADD-Friendly Ways to Get Organized.* New York: Taylor and Francis, Imprint of Brunner-Routledge, 2002.

Lehmkuhl, Dorothy, and Dolores Catter Lamping. *Organizing for the Creative Person*. New York: Crown Trade Paperbacks, 1993.

Organizations

National Association for Professional Organizers (NAPO)
Phone: 512-206-0151

National Study Group on the Chronically Disorganized
Judith Kolberg, Director
Phone: 404-231-6172

How to Contact Professionals Quoted in This Book

Mary Crouch, organizer
Phone: 734-930-9286
E-mail: mail4mary111@aol.com

Hope Langner, coach
Phone: 518-439-2467
Web site: hlanger@nycap.rr.com

Andrea Little, consultant
Web site: Annie12345@aol.com

Nancy Ratey, coach
Phone: 781-237-3508
Web site: www.nancyratey.com

Susan Sussman, Director
American Coaching Association (ACA)
Phone: 610-825-8572
Web site: www.americoach.com

Your Self in the World

Other Helpful Books for the Journey

Hallowell, Edward, M.D. *Connect*. New York: Pantheon Books, 1999.
_____. *Human Moments: How to Find Meaning and Love in Your Everyday Life*. Health Communications, 2001.

Katherine, Anne. *Where to Draw the Line: How to Set Healthy Boundaries Every Day*. New York: Simon & Schuster, 2000.

Lerner, Harriet Goldhor. *The Dance of Anger*. New York: Harper & Row, 1985, 1989.
_____. *The Dance of Connection: How to Talk to Someone When You're Mad, Hurt, Scared, Frustrated, Insulted, Betrayed, or Desperate*. New York: HarperCollins, 2001.
_____. *The Dance of Intimacy*. New York: Harper & Row, 1985, 1989.

Stone, Douglas, Bruce Patton, and Sheila Heen. *Difficult Conversations: How to Discuss What Matters Most*. New York: Viking Penguin, 1999.

Payson, Eleanor. *The Wizard of Oz and Other Narcissists*. Julian Day Publications, 2002 (to order, contact www.eleanorpayson.com)

Pipher, Mary. *Reviving Ophelia: Saving the Selves of Adolescent Girls*. New York: Ballantine Books, 1994.

Ratey, John, M.D. *User's Guide to the Brain: Personality, Behavior, and the Four Theaters of the Brain (Age of Unreason)*. New York: Pantheon Books, 2001.

Ratey, John, M.D., and Catherine Johnson. *Shadow Syndromes*. New York: Pantheon Books, 1997.

Sher, B. *Live the Life You Love*. New York: Dell, 1996.

Viorst, Judith. *Necessary Losses: The Loves, Illusions, Dependencies, and Impossible Expectations That All of Us Have to Give Up in Order to Grow*. New York: Ballantine Books, 1986.

West. Thomas G. *In the Mind's Eye: Visual Thinkers, Gifted People with Dyslexia and Other Learning Difficulties, Compter Images and the Ironies of Creativity*. New York: Prometheus Books, 1991, 1997.

Acknowledgments

I RECENTLY READ A BOOK BY Stephen King called *On Writing* in which he describes the writing practices of a variety of writers. He tells a story about James Joyce, who apparently struggled and labored over every word he wrote. Supposedly one day when a friend came to visit Joyce, he found him hunched over his writing desk looking pained. Knowing of his difficulties, the friend inquired how many words he had written that day. When Joyce answered that he had written seven words, his friend said encouragingly, "That's very good for you, James." "Yes," agreed Joyce, "but now I have to decide what order to put them in!"

This story resonated with me as it might for anyone with AD/HD trying to write and then put in order as many words as this book contains. It is a task for which I have many people to thank.

Thank you, thank you, thank you to John Fulton, a gifted and patient editor who worked so long and hard for and with me to help put my thoughts in order.

I want to thank John Ratey for referring me to Jill Kneerim, who eventually became my agent. And I want to thank Jill for patiently and expertly helping me develop and express my ideas.

Special thanks to Jackie Johnson, my editor at Walker & Company, who understood and appreciated my message and worked with me so expertly and calmly to help me make this book what I wanted it to be. And thank you to George Gibson and Jackie for taking a chance on another AD/HD book that I promised would be different. My thanks also goes to the entire staff at Walker & Company all of whom have been so supportive and warm during this process, with special thanks to Vicki Haire for adding polish and clarity to the text.

I will be forever grateful to Tim Underwood at Underwood Books for helping launch me into this world of writing about adult AD/HD, a world that has brought me so many opportunities to connect with wonderful people all over the world.

Writing a book when you have AD/HD requires a great deal of support and a belief in the value of interdependence, as well as an understanding of how each person in a system plays such an important role in the lives of the other members of that group. So I want to thank a lot of people.

First I want to acknowledge and thank my office and life support staff. My great appreciation and gratitude to Denise Brogdon for her incredibly nonjudgmental, supportive, and superior work. Also, thanks to Mary Morgan for her wonderful help as well. To Barb Osga and Tuncheller Brooks, thank you for your personal support. What a team! Your wonderful help orders the world around me, allowing me to focus on this kind of work.

Thank you to my friends and colleagues in the world of adult AD/HD for the kind of friendship, support, and camaraderie that I've never found anything quite like anywhere else. In addition to those I thanked in my first book, I also want to mention by name John and Nancy Ratey, Ellen Littman, Hope Langner, Sue Sussman, Thom and Louise Hartman, Geri Markel, Art Robin, Kate Kelly, Peggy Ramundo, Roger Lauer, Ellie Payson, and, of course, Ned Hallowell for their professional and personal support over the last few years—in times of controversy as well as celebration they were by my side, and I want them to know what a difference that made to me. I want to thank ADDA (National Attention Deficit Disorder Association) for its continuing support of my work, as well as Wilma Fellman and everyone in MAAAN (Michigan Adolescent and Adult AD/HD Network for Professionals).

I want to acknowledge and thank those talented people who are responsible for the beautiful artwork and graphics in the book. This includes Howard Morris, Genia Service, and David Zinn.

Thank you to Abe and Roselle Sperling, who provided such a nurturing and peaceful environment for me to spend a very special summer writing and "swimming with the frogs." Thanks to Barbara Devanney, who started this project with me that summer and helped get me over that first hump.

And here's to my friends De-De and Chi-Chi, whom I dearly miss. They have given me an awareness of how important it is to appreciate people you care about while they are still here to listen. So while I have the chance I want to thank people whose personal support and friendship have enriched my life over the last few years. Thank you to Lori Saginaw, Karen Morgan, Jill and Tom Koepke, Annie and Rob Cohen and Marcie Bell, and Bruce Victor.

Thanks to Natasha for sending me that little photo one day and saying "I think this girl looks like your daughter."

Also, thanks to Terra Webster, Melissa Linick, and Sandy Heywood. Without all of your support I would not have been able to focus and complete this work while at the same time keeping a happy family balance.

And of course I want to thank my family. My father, David Shubow, who passed away in 1998. He wanted me to call this book "Everything I have learned about AD/HD since my last book." Well, Dad, even though the title is different, this is what the book really is about. Thank you for teaching me by example and word everything you knew about the creative process and about taking the road less taken. Thank you to my mother, Marion Shubow, for her unfailing support and great encouragement and interest in my work. And to Jennifer English and Josephine Small for their incredible support and loyalty and care, which affected our entire family. I also want to express love and appreciation to my brother, Mike. And I want to express gratitude to my husband, Dean's, family for their love and acceptance of my uniqueness.

Thank you to my children, Evan and Dasha, who have filled my heart with love as well as given me such an appreciation of the gifts that differences can bring.

And then, of course, I especially want to express my deep love and appreciation to Dean for his constant love, friendship, support, help, patience, and acceptance, as well as for being by my side during so many AD/HD events over the years, events at which he has made such a unique and meaningful contribution of his own.

I thank you all.

Index